THE 13 STEPS TO RICHES

BASED ON THE WORK BY NAPOLEON HILL IN THINK AND GROW RICH

CREATED BY MULTI #1 INTERNATIONAL BESTSELLING AUTHOR & AWARD WINNING SPEAKER ON HABITS

ERIK "MR AWESOME" SWANSON

THE
13 STEPS TO
RICHES

Featuring
Erik Swanson & John Assaraf

#1 BESTSELLER

THE BRAIN
VOLUME 12

HABITUDE
WARRIOR

Foreword by Dr. Steve Taubman

Manufactured and printed in the United States of America and distributed globally by Beyond Publishing and Integrity Publishing International.

Hardback ISBN: 978-1-964330-21-1
Paperback ISBN: 978-1-964330-20-4

TESTIMONIALS
THE 13 STEPS TO RICHES

"What an honor to collaborate with so many personal development leaders from around the world as we Co-Author together honoring the amazing principles by Napoleon Hill in this new book series, *The 13 Steps to Riches*, by Habitude Warrior and Erik "Mr. Awesome" Swanson. Well done, "Mr. Awesome," for putting together such an amazing series. If you want to up-level your life, read every book in this series and learn to apply each of these time-tested steps and principles."

Denis Waitley ~ Author of *Psychology of Winning & The NEW Psychology of Winning—Top Qualities of a 21st Century Winner*

"Just as *Think and Grow Rich* reveals the 13 steps to success discovered by Napoleon Hill after interviewing the richest people around the world (and many who considered themselves failures) in the early 1900s, *The 13 Steps to Riche*s, produced by Habitude Warrior and Erik Swanson takes a modern look at those same 13 steps. It brings together many of today's personal development leaders to share their stories of how *The 13 Steps to Riches* have created and propelled their own successes. I am honored to participate and share the power of Faith in my life. If you truly want to accelerate reaching the success you deserve, read every volume of *The 13 Steps to Riches*."

Sharon Lechter ~ 5 Time N.Y. Times Bestselling Author. Author of *Think and Grow Rich for Women*, Co-Author of *Exit Rich*, *Rich Dad Poor Dad*, *Three Feet from Gold*, *Outwitting the Devil* and *Success and Something Greater*

"The most successful book on personal achievement ever written is now being elaborated upon by many of the world's top thought leaders. I'm honored to Co-Author this series on the amazing principles from Napoleon Hill, in *The 13 Steps to Riches*, by Habitude Warrior, Erik "Mr. Awesome" Swanson."

> *Jim Cathcart* ~ Bestselling Author of *Relationship Selling* and *The Acorn Principle*, among many others. Certified Speaking Professional (CSP) and Former President of the National Speakers Association (NSA)

"Some books are written to be read and placed on the shelf. Others are written to transform the reader, as they travel down a path of true transcendence and enlightenment. *The 13 Steps to Riches* by Habitude Warrior and Erik Swanson is the latter. Profoundly insightful, it revitalizes the techniques and strategies written by Napoleon Hill by applying a modern perspective, and a fearsome collaboration of some of the greatest minds and thought leaders from around the globe. A must-read for all of those who seek to break free of their current levels of success, and truly extract the greatness that lies within. It is an honor and a privilege to have been selected to participate, in what is destined to be the next historic chapter in the meteoric rise of many men and women around the world."

> *Glenn Lundy* ~ Husband to one, Father to 8, Automotive Industry Expert, Author of *The Morning 5*, Creator of the popular morning show "#riseandgrind," and the Founder of "Breakfast With Champions"

"How exciting to team up with the amazing Habitude Warrior community of leaders such as Erik Swanson, Sharon Lechter, John Assaraf, Denis Waitley and so many more transformational and self-help icons to bring you these timeless and proven concepts in the fields of success and wealth. *The 13 Steps to Riches* book series will help you reach your dreams and accomplish your goals faster than you have ever experienced before!"

> *Dame Marie Diamond* ~ Featured in *The Secret*, Modern-Day Spiritual Teacher, Inspirational Speaker, Feng Shui Master

"If you are looking to crystalize your mightiest dream, rekindle your passion, break through limiting beliefs and learn from those who have done exactly what you want to do—read this book! In this transformational masterpiece, *The 13 Steps to Riches*, self-development guru Erik Swanson has collected the sage wisdom and time-tested truths from subject matter experts and amalgamated it into a one-stop-shop resource library that will change your life forever!"

Dan Clark ~ Speaker Hall of Fame & N.Y. Times Bestselling Author of *The Art of Significance*

"Life has always been about who you surround yourself with. I am in excellent company with this collaboration from my fellow authors and friends, paying tribute to the life-changing principles by Napoleon Hill in this amazing new book series, *The 13 Steps to Riches*, organized by Habitude Warrior's founder and my dear friend, Erik Swanson. Hill said, 'Your big opportunity may be right where you are now.' This book series is a must-read for anyone who wants to change their lives and prosper, starting now."

Alec Stern ~ America's Startup Success Expert, Co-Founder of Constant Contact

"Finally a book series that encompasses the lessons the world needs to learn and apply, but in our modern day era. As I always teach my students to "Say YES, and then figure out how," I strongly urge you to do the same. Say YES to adding all of these 13 books in *The 13 Steps to Riches* book series into your success library and watch both your business as well as your personal life grow as a result."

Loral Langemeier ~ 5 Time N.Y. Times Bestselling Author, Featured in *The Secret*, Author of *The Millionaire Maker* and *YES! Energy - The Equation to Do Less, Make More*

"Napoleon Hill had a tremendous impact on my consciousness when I was very young – there were very few books nor the type of trainings that we see today to lead us to success. Whenever you have the opportunity to read and harness *The 13 Steps to Riches* as they are presented in this series, be happy (and thankful) that there were many of us out there applying the principles, testing the teachings, making the mistakes, and now being offered to you in a way that they are clear, simple and concise—with samples and distinctions that will make it easier for you to design a successful life which includes adding value to others, solving world problems, and making the world work for 100% of humanity... Read on... those dreams are about to come true!"

Dame Doria Cordova ~ CEO of Money & You, Excellerated Business School, Global Business Developer, Ambassador of New Education

"Success leaves clues and the Co-Authors in this awesome book series, *The 13 Steps to Riches*, will continue the Napoleon Hill legacy with tools, tips and modern-day principals that greatly expand on the original masterpiece... *Think and Grow Rich*. If you are serious about living your life to the max, get this book series now!"

John Assaraf ~ Chairman & CEO NeuroGym, MrNeuroGym.com, N.Y. Times Bestselling author of *Having It All*, *Innercise*, and *The Answer*. Also featured in *The Secret*

"Over the years, I have been blessed with many rare and amazing opportunities to invest my time and energy. These opportunities require a keen eye and immediate action. This is one of those amazing opportunities for you as a reader! I highly recommend you pick up every book in this series of *The 13 Steps to Riches* by Habitude Warrior and Erik Swanson! Learn from modern-day leaders who have embraced the lessons from the great Napoleon Hill in his classic book from 1937, *Think and Grow Rich*."

Kevin Harrington ~ Original "Shark" on Shark Tank, Creator of the Infomercial, Pioneer of the 'As Seen on TV' brand, Co-Author of *Mentor to Millions*

"When you begin your journey, you will quickly learn of the importance of the first step of *The 13 Steps To Riches*. A burning desire is the start of all worthwhile achievements. Erik 'Mr. Awesome' Swanson's newest book series contains a wealth of assistance to make your journey both successful and enjoyable. Start today... because tomorrow is not guaranteed on your calendar."

Don Green ~ 45 Years of Banking, Finance & Entrepreneurship, Bestselling Author of *Everything I Know About Success I Learned From Napoleon Hill & Napoleon Hill My Mentor: Timeless Principles to Take Your Success to the Next Level & Your Millionaire Mindset*

Our minds become magnetized with the dominating thoughts we hold in our minds and these magnets attract to us the forces, the people, the circumstances of life which harmonize with the nature of our dominating thoughts.

(Napoleon Hill)

Global Speakers Mastermind & Habitude Warrior Masterminds

Join us and become a member of our tribe! Our Global Speakers Mastermind is a virtual group of amazing thinkers and leaders who meet twice a month. Sessions are designed to be 'to the point' and focused while sharing fantastic techniques to grow your mindset as well as your pocketbooks. We also include famous guest speaker spots for our private Masterclasses. We also designate certain sessions for our members to mastermind with each other & and counsel on the topics discussed in our previous Masterclasses. It's time for you to join a tribe who truly cares about **YOU** and your future and start surrounding yourself with the famous leaders and mentors of our time. It is time for you to up-level your life, businesses, and relationships.

For more information to check out our Masterminds:
Team@HabitudeWarrior.com
www.DecideToBeAwesome.com

BECOME AN INTERNATIONAL
#1 BESTSELLING AUTHOR & SPEAKER

Habitude Warrior International has been highlighting award-winning Speakers and #1 Bestselling Authors for over 25 years. They know what it takes to become #1 in your field and how to get the best exposure around the world. If you have ever considered giving yourself the GIFT of becoming a well-known Speaker and a fantastically well known #1 Best-Selling Author, then you should email their team right away to find out more information in how you can become involved. They have the best of the best when it comes to resources in achieving the bestselling status in your particular field. Start surrounding yourself with the N.Y. Times Bestsellers of our time and start seeing your dreams become reality!

For more information to become a #1 Bestselling Author
& Speaker on our Habitude Warrior Conferences
Please text the word AUTHORS to 619-304-6268
And also go to:
www.DecideToBeAwesome.com

Acknowledgement To Napoleon Hill

I would like to personally acknowledge and thank the one and only Napoleon Hill for his work, dedication, and most importantly believing in himself. His unwavering belief in himself, whether he realized this or not, had been passed down from generation to generation to millions and millions of individuals across this planet including me!

I'm sure, at first, as many of us experience throughout our lives as well, he most likely had his doubts. Think about it. Being offered to work for Andrew Carnegie for a full twenty years with zero pay and no guarantee of success had to be a daunting decision. But, I thank you for making that decision years and years ago. It paved the path for countless many who have trusted in themselves and found success in their own rights. You gave us all hope, desire, and faith to bank on the most important energy in the world—ourselves!

For this, I thank you Sir, from the bottom of my heart and the top of all of our bank accounts. Let us all follow the 13 Steps to Riches and prosper in so many areas of our lives.

~ Erik "Mr. Awesome" Swanson
13 Time #1 Bestselling Author & Student of Napoleon Hill Philosophies

Navy Corpsman Maxton W. Soviak, 22

It is our distinct honor to dedicate each one of *The 13 Steps to Riches* book volumes to each of the 13 United States Service Members who courageously lost their lives in Kabul in August 2021. Your honor, dignity, and strength will always be cherished and remembered.

~ Habitude Warrior Team

Navy Corpsman Maxton W. Soviak, 22, of Berlin Heights, Ohio.

Assigned to 1st Marine Regiment, 1st Marine Division, Camp Pendleton, California. His awards and decorations include the National Defense Service Medal, Good Conduct Medal, and Flag Letter of Accommodation. Additional awards pending approval may include Purple Heart, Combat Action Ribbon, and Sea Service Deployment Ribbon. We honor you and thank you for your ultimate sacrifice!

THE 13 FEATURED CELEBRITY AUTHORS

DENIS WAITLEY ~ Author of *Psychology of Winning* & *The NEW Psychology of Winning—Top Qualities of a 21st Century Winner*, NASA's Performance Coach, Featured in *The Secret.* ~ www.DenisWaitley.com

SHARON LECHTER ~ Five Time N.Y. Times Bestselling Author. Author of *Think and Grow Rich for Women*, Co-Author of *Exit Rich, Rich Dad Poor Dad, Three Feet from Gold, Outwitting the Devil* and *Success and Something Greater.* ~ www.SharonLechter.com

JIM CATHCART ~ Bestselling Author of *Relationship Selling* and *The Acorn Principle*, among many others. Certified Speaking Professional (CSP) and Former President of the National Speakers Association (NSA). ~ www.Cathcart.com

MICHAEL E. GERBER ~ N.Y. Times Bestseller of the mega-bestselling theory for over two consecutive decades... *The E-Myth* Books. ~ www.MichaelEGerberCompanies.com

GLENN LUNDY ~ Husband to one, Father to eight, Automotive Industry Expert, Author of *The Morning 5*, Creator of the popular morning show "#riseandgrind," and the Founder of Breakfast With Champions. ~ www.GlennLundy.com

MARIE DIAMOND ~ Featured in *The Secret*, Modern Day Spiritual Teacher, Inspirational Speaker, Feng Shui Master. ~ www.MarieDiamond.com

DAN CLARK ~ Award Winning Speaker, Speaker Hall of Fame, N.Y. Times Bestselling Author of *The Art of Significance.*
~ www.DanClark.com

ALEC STERN ~ America's Startup Success Expert, Co-Founder of Constant Contact, Speaker, Mentor, and Investor. ~ www.AlecSpeaks.com

ERIK SWANSON ~ 13 Time #1 International Bestselling Author, Award-Winning Speaker, Featured on TEDx Talks and Amazon Prime TV. Founder and CEO of the Habitude Warrior Brand. ~ www.SpeakerErikSwanson.com

LORAL LANGEMEIER ~ Five Time N.Y. Times Bestselling Author, Featured in *The Secret*, Author of *The Millionaire Maker* and *YES! Energy - The Equation to Do Less, Make More.* ~ www.LoralLangemeier.com

DORIA CORDOVA ~ CEO of Money & You, Excellerated Business School, Global Business Developer, Ambassador of New Education.
~ www.FridaysWithDoria.com

JOHN ASSARAF ~ Chairman & CEO NeuroGym, MrNeuroGym.com, New York Times Bestselling Author of *Having It All*, *Innercise*, and *The Answer*. Also featured in *The Secret*. ~ www.JohnAssaraf.com

 **KEVIN HARRINGTON** ~ Original "Shark" on the hit TV show Shark Tank, Creator of the Infomercial, Pioneer of the As Seen on TV brand, Co-Author of *Mentor to Millions*. ~ www.KevinHarrington.TV

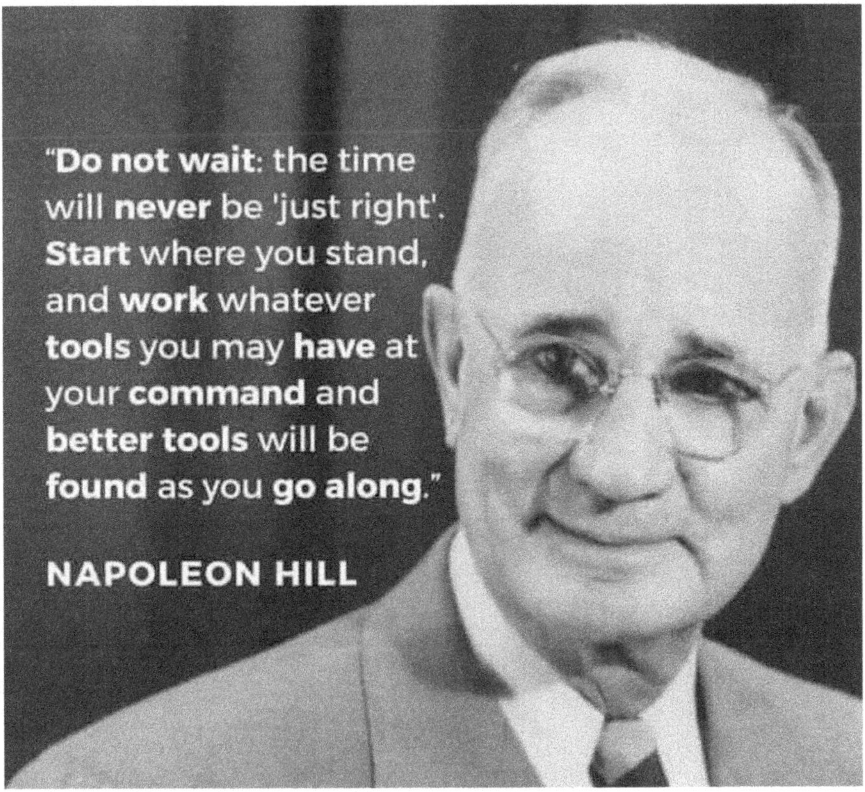

"**Do not wait**: the time will **never** be 'just right'. **Start** where you stand, and **work** whatever **tools** you may **have** at your **command** and **better tools** will be **found** as you **go along**."

NAPOLEON HILL

CONTENTS

ERIK SWANSON & DON GREEN

Once you give yourself the gift of reading Erik Swanson's newest book series, *The 13 Steps to Riches*, you are sure to realize why he has earned his nickname, "*Mr. Awesome.*" Readers usually read books for two reasons – they want to be entertained or they want to improve their knowledge in a certain subject. Mr. Awesome's new book series will help you do both.

I urge you to not only read this great book series in it's entirety, but also apply the principles held within into your our life. Use the experience Erik Swanson has gained to reach your own level of success. I highly encourage you to invest in yourself by reading self-help materials, such as *The 13 Steps to Riches*, and I truly know you will discover that it will be one of the best investments you could ever make.

Don Green
Executive Director and CEO
The Napoleon Hill Foundation

FOREWORD
BY DR. STEVE TAUBMAN

I've been teaching personal development principles for over three decades. I've made my living writing books and speaking to audiences about success, leadership, resilience, creativity, and self-awareness. I've helped thousands to live abundant lives, and I've been blessed to enjoy great success while making a difference—something I wish for you as well, dear reader!

One thing I've learned from my lifetime study of the mind and the brain is that there's no way you'll ever be "fixed." No matter how much effort you've made to release your past, cultivate emotional intelligence, develop mindfulness, or push through your challenges, you're most likely going to have slips. You might feel at times, despite your best efforts, depression, anxiety, grief, and even confusion. You may even come to believe some very disempowering thoughts about yourself. And you may even suffer.

How do I know this? Because I'm one of the people you've read, watched, and listened to for years, and I go through periods like this myself. And here's a little secret. I would venture to say that many of the authors in this book have as well. And how do I know this? Because for many years, I've had the honor of sharing stages and platforms with many speakers and authors. We are all human.

So, if even some of the experts suffer, what's the point of learning this stuff?

Very simply, perspective!

I've come to be known as the teacher who says, "Don't believe everything you think." We tend to accept every negative thought that enters our minds, rather than the preferred route of maintaining wisdom and perspective when that part of our mind is trying to convince us that whatever we're thinking is true and must be thought of now. We have to rise above the "egoic mind."

But how do we accomplish that? How do you weather the negative storm when your mind is trying to convince you that you're unworthy, flawed, hopeless, or doomed?

Enter the authors of this amazing book. Great minds like that of John Assaraf and Erik Swanson have been illuminating the path to self-awareness, consciousness, optimism, and inner peace for many years. I've learned from everyone in this book. And I'd like to think that they've learned from me as well.

A friend of mine says, "None of us are as smart as all of us" and "You can't be your best self by yourself." These are powerful words that remind us that, when we're steeped in illusion, suffering from a lack of perspective, we can find solace in the words of wise souls who might have suffered themselves and have developed tools, methods, attitudes, and perspectives that have helped them move beyond that suffering.

We all want and need perspective. We all require a beacon of light now and then; some more than others.

Let the people you meet on these pages serve as that beacon. Let their wisdom and knowledge that they share displace the negative, disempowering, painful, yet fundamentally false views that may live inside of you and in all of us. And let them show you how to cultivate strength, self-confidence, resilience, joy, and hope.

We all fall down. But the tools you will learn here, like John Assaraf's eloquent treatise on negative self-talk or Erik Swanson's clear and optimistic explanations of the neurology of belief, can and will help you stand back up more quickly and remind you that whatever you think that isn't in your highest and best good is dead wrong.

You have what it takes to succeed. Your marvelous brain is the perfect instrument for the life you seek, even if you've come to be absolutely convinced that you're beyond help.

Here are a few things to remember as you navigate the path to befriending your brain and embracing a better life. Watch for them in these pages:

- The truth is beautiful, so if what you're experiencing isn't beautiful, it isn't truth.

- Don't suffer over your suffering. Pain is inevitable, but suffering is optional.

- Try this mantra: Dissolve illusion. Illuminate truth.

- Learn to be the loving observer of your own experience.

- The mind is like a muscle. With exercise, its strength will change your trajectory.

- No matter how hopeless things seem, transformation is closer than you think. Winston Churchill said, "Everything is impossible until it's done."

- Grade yourself on a curve. If your mind gives you a C, assume it's really a B. When it gives you a B, it's probably an A.

- Stop accepting the default thoughts that arise in your mind and let the experts here show you how to replace disempowering thoughts with empowering ones.

- And finally, when part of you says this is all untrue, that you ARE hopeless and DO deserve the harsh judgments your mind is foisting on you, remember that's just your mind doing what minds do. But luckily, you can take control of your mind.

I'm excited for you. In these pages, you'll not only learn that you are far more than your mind, but you'll discover tools and exercises that will allow you to experience that reality for yourself; to have a felt sense of this truth.

These are not mere platitudes. Lurking beneath the habitual and often damaging workings of your egoic mind is a fountain of hope and brilliance and possibility that will bring you to a new level of awareness, empowering you to make your life and that of those around you infinitely better.

Go forth, learn, peel away the layers of illusion, make a difference, rejoice in your greatness… and don't believe everything you think!

With peace and gratitude,

Dr. Steve Taubman
Author of *UnHypnosis, Bulletproof,* and *Buddha in the Trenches*

DR. STEVE TAUBMAN

Dr. Steve's early years were plagued by crippling anxiety, depression, and low self-esteem. Despite graduating valedictorian from one of the nation's top chiropractic colleges and running a thriving practice, Dr. Steve found that his outer success did little to calm his inner turmoil.

Thus began a thirty-year journey to understand the root of happiness. His exploration of Western psychotherapy, Eastern teachings of mindfulness, hypnosis, and the science of prosperity provided profound insight into the universal nature and cause of suffering; the subconscious mind… which ultimately led to the creation of his successful *UnHypnosis* system and bestselling book.

Blending his teachings with a long-time passion for humor and magic, Dr. Steve developed a series of insightful, fun presentations about mastering the subconscious mind which was quickly embraced by organizations for their ability to get people in action.

Since then, Dr. Steve's excitement, motivation, and enthusiasm have earned him fans from every profession as he continues to enthrall audiences worldwide, helping them remove mental barriers to achieving their dreams.

An avid outdoor enthusiast, Steve currently resides in Vermont with his dog, Ernie, where he is close to hiking, skiing, and biking. As a licensed pilot, he often flies himself to and from his engagements.

A deeply spiritual individual, Steve especially loves helping people translate their spiritual principles into useful tools for their day-to-day lives.

www.SteveTaubman.com

John Assaraf

YOUR BRAIN & SELF-LIMITING BELIEFS: THE GOOD, THE BAD, & THE UGLY

If no one had told you otherwise, would you believe that the Earth was flat, the stars were celestial beings, and beyond the horizon, the sea dropped off into oblivion?

If you're like most modern people, you have other ideas in mind.

A spherical Earth spins on an axis; the planets revolve around the Sun. Stars aren't gods of fire—they're luminous spheroids of plasma. If a crowd of people were to try to convince you otherwise, you'd have centuries of scientific evidence to prove them wrong.

But what if, when you woke up each morning, you assumed that nothing much existed beyond your horizon?

What if every time you saw yourself in the mirror, your reflection echoed back: "You're neither smart nor spectacular enough to succeed," and "You're too unlucky to ever be loved?"

Would you let those beliefs prevent you from setting sail to see what truly lies on your horizon?

Take 'em to Task

Sadly, there's no peer review in your head to fact-check any ideas you may have of yourself. There's no objective eye in your prefrontal cortex to test the validity of the hypotheses you've formed about your life, the universe, and everything.

It's all too easy to turn conjectures into conclusions. Theories into dogma. Impressions into judgments.

A statement like "I'm worthless," "I'm unlovable," or "I'm doomed to failure" might sound harmless if you say it once. But words have a way of persuading even unbelievers if you repeat them often enough. You may find yourself cherry-picking memories from your personal history to prove to yourself that the beliefs you hold in the present are true.

Call it negative self-talk or self-flagellation. The devil on your shoulder. None of us have escaped the clutches of self-limiting beliefs. They creep up when we're about to step out of our comfort zone. They may pull us into cowardice when we feel brave enough to follow a dream. They often lurk below the field of awareness, which makes them even more insidious.

Scientists have been trained to scrutinize any theory they have about the universe.

Isn't it time to take your negative self-talk to task?

What the Bleep's Behind a Belief?

What goes on in your brain when you believe—in a benevolent creator of the universe, in life after death, or in damnation, for that matter? Why, from the perspective of the evolution of cognition, do human beings form belief systems—like religion—in the first place?

Social scientists ask why cultures transmit systems of belief: Why do native Polynesians see spirits in the waves and Catholics feel certain of the Holy Trinity? Biologists see beliefs as traits of evolution: Which social and emotional interactions have led to their formation?

To neuroscientists, beliefs run deeper than the culture or the social and environmental contexts. They represent complex brain-based phenomena that form the basis of all social exchanges and moral intuitions.

The Good

When you trust in the goodness of your neighbors, it enables you to participate in community life, and to form healthy social bonds. Without community, you might find it difficult to thrive, let alone survive, in the world. Unless your neighbors prove otherwise, it's healthy for your brain to believe that they're decent people.

Moreover, a belief in karma, or "what goes around comes around," also encourages neighbors to act ethically towards each other. Codes of behavior, at their best, help people to live in relative peace.

The Bad

Beliefs also offer people a way to cope when difficult things happen in life. They help humans to accept misfortune. If you grow up with a cat, and that cat gets hit by a bus, it's comforting to believe in an animal heaven. When a volcano erupts, a belief in a just but fiery god can help people to make sense of devastation.

The Ugly

Along the same lines, when you say to yourself, "I'm unworthy," your brain might be looking for an easy way to make sense of personal misfortune. Although the human brain is a complex and intricately fascinating organ—it's also lazy. If your brain can operate with minimal effort, it will. Thinking that you're unworthy of love may be the quickest pathway your brain has found to protect you from the losses and disappointments inherent in intimate human relationships.

Where in the Brain is Belief?

Some neuroscientists hypothesize that specific patterns of brain activity play different roles in the art of believing. Some beliefs engage posterior regions of the brain, while others engage areas involved in abstract reasoning. Whenever you believe anything about yourself—whether it's "I'm a mess" or "I'm the best thing since sliced bread," you engage brain networks involved in memory retrieval and imagery.

The default mode network, or what some researchers call "the imagination network," plays a central role in formulating and maintaining beliefs about who you think you are. It's the network that governs all your autobiographical memories. It daydreams about who you might have been in the past and who you think you might be in the future.

The more you recall ideas and feelings about yourself, the stronger the neural pathways that carry those memories will get. That process is what forms your self-concept; it's what builds your identity. Freud referred to the whole thing as the "ego."

Whatever you call it, a consistent belief in who you are as a person also has an evolutionary purpose. Without a stable sense of self, life would be a helluva thing to navigate.

Aye, There's the Rub

Now, this may be hard to believe—but every belief you have about yourself is "self-limiting."

Do you believe that you are good? Bad? Ugly?

Whatever you believe and however you believe it, you're putting limits around who you truly are. As Shakespeare's Hamlet says in Act 2, Scene 2: "There is nothing either good or bad, but thinking makes it so."

If you think you are a "good" person, that belief may be preventing you from appreciating the full spectrum of your personality. Believing in your unassailable goodness can lead to all forms of denial. But if you believe yourself to be a "bad" person, is it any better?

What's the Solution? Innercise!

Train your brain to keep those self-limiting beliefs from running wild and unverified in your mind. Just as you wouldn't drink milk past its due date, don't swallow ideas about yourself just because they're sitting on the front shelf of your brain!

You exercise your leg muscles when you walk an extra mile. Now walk an extra mile in your mind. Innercise the "muscles" (or synapses) that form your neural pathways, so they remain agile, responsive, and awake.

Expand your potential for deeper levels of awareness. Whenever your default mode network starts stirring up beliefs about who you think you are, notice those beliefs for what they are.

But first, take a moment and notice the pattern of your breathing. Is it quick? Soft? Labored?

Whatever you're experiencing, let go of any judgment.

Notice your physical body in the present. If it helps, gently caress the palms of your hands. Experience pleasure without judgment, blame, shame, guilt, or justification, in this moment. Let go of any beliefs of who you think you might be right now. If beliefs arise, just notice them dispassionately.

When you feel relaxed and steady in your body and mind, tap into your wise inner voice (or your expert innerciser, if you prefer).

Ask your expert innerciser: What beliefs do I harbor about myself that are reigning in my true self? Are any of my beliefs holding me back from living fully? Are any of my ideas about who I am inhibiting me from meeting my potential? From reaching my goals?

Write down those beliefs.

Now read them back. Slowly. Calmly.

Recognize that whatever you're reading is something you've taken part in constructing. It's all fabrication. And if it's limiting you now, you have the power to let the story go.

When you achieve a little distance from those self-limiting beliefs, recognize and relish in having freedom from them. The more you do this, the more it will become a habit and the more natural it will feel to sit in the driver's seat in front of an open road.

In this space of freedom, it's your call. It's your turn. Hands on the wheel.

Choose to believe something new about yourself. Go down a different road. Play a different part in your own life. Believe in your self-worth, your beauty, and your potential. Whatever you wish.

Do you believe that you can meet your financial goals this year? Why not? What's holding you back? Is it something tangible? Can you name the limitations you're putting on your financial freedom? Write those barriers down and see them for what they are.

Do the same for any goal you may have, whether it's love, work, or travel. Check in next week as we tackle the neuroscience of goal setting and achievement.

Now that you know a little bit more about what self-limiting beliefs are, isn't it easier to just sail past them?

JOHN ASSARAF

John Assaraf, "The Brain Whisperer," is one of the leading high-performance success coaches in the world. He is a behavioral neuroscience researcher who has appeared numerous times on *Larry King Live*, *Anderson Cooper*, and *The Ellen DeGeneres Show*.

As CEO and co-founder, he grew RE/MAX of Indiana from startup to 85 offices and 1200 sales associates who sold over $4 Billion a year.

John was also one of the founders of Bamboo/IPIX, which went public on NASDAQ with a market cap of $2.5 Billion.

John has written four books, including two New York Times bestsellers that have been translated into thirty-five languages. He is the creator of the *Innercise* movement and has been featured in eleven movies, including the blockbuster hit *The Secret* and *Quest For Success* with Richard Branson and the Dalai Lama.

He lives in San Diego with his wife and two sons. In addition to being a vegan, meditator, an avid skier, and ocean lover, he loves traveling the world and making some of the tastiest hot sauces using some of the hottest peppers on the planet.

Today, he is CEO of *MyNeuroGym.com*, a neuroscience-based company dedicated to helping individuals strengthen their mindset so they achieve their goals and dreams… faster and easier than ever before.

www.JohnAssaraf.com

Erik Swanson

EVERYTHING IS LEARNABLE

"The key to success is to focus our conscious mind on things we desire, not things we fear. Everything is learnable, and what others have learned, you can learn as well. To earn more, you must learn more. Our goal is not to change everyone, but to change those that are ready for change."
~ Brian Tracy

Ladies and gentlemen and curious minds, allow me to share a perspective with you. I believe everything is learnable!

The brightest minds in history have all shown us that our brain power is much more powerful than our brawn power. It's also well known that each of these brilliant minds have all been considered "crazy" as well. It's the crazy ones who take chances, risks, and try things, who seem to make those breakthroughs, invent something innovative, and contribute to the world forever and ever.

Guess what? My theory is that everything is learnable. This is an amazing concept and means that if someone else had done it before you, you can do it, too!

There's a great story about a runner from England named Roger Bannister. In 1954, Roger was the very first person to ever run a sub-four-minute mile. He came in at three minutes and fifty-nine seconds. This was huge. But, the huge part of the story was yet to come. He held his world record for exactly forty-six days, until someone else beat it... and then another, and another.

The moral of the story is that once people realized it was possible, they all started to train their brains. Just the mere realization that it was possible was enough for people to start breaking that threshold. They all started to keep these positive thoughts of victory in the forefront of their minds. It works!

Benefit By Tapping into Your Brain Power

Picture a classroom without walls, where the curriculum extends beyond textbooks and lectures. I believe that every experience, challenge, and encounter is a lesson waiting to be absorbed. From the intricacies of quantum physics to the nuances of human emotions, the canvas of learning is ever-expanding.

In the symphony of learning, no subject is too complex, no skill too elusive. As we traverse the landscape of knowledge, let us do so with the unwavering belief that everything is within our grasp. The realization of this concept opens up the doors to the world for all of us.

The brain plays a crucial role in our self-development, encompassing various cognitive processes, emotional regulation, and learning mechanisms.

Key Factors in How the Brain Contributes to Self-Development

- **Neuroplasticity:** The brain has the ability to reorganize itself by forming new neural connections throughout life. This process, known as euro plasticity, allows individuals to adapt to experiences, learn new skills, and overcome challenges.

- **Learning & Memory:** The brain's capacity to acquire, process, and store information is fundamental to self-development. Learning involves changes in synaptic connections, and memory allows individuals to retain and retrieve knowledge, experiences, and skills that contribute to personal growth.

- **Emotional Regulation:** Different brain regions, such as the amygdala and prefrontal cortex, play crucial roles in emotional processing and regulation. Self-development often involves understanding and managing emotions, which relies on the brain's ability to regulate emotional responses and make informed decisions.

- **Executive Functions:** The prefrontal cortex is associated with executive functions, including decision-making, planning, problem-solving, and impulse control. These functions are essential for setting goals, making choices, and navigating life in a purposeful manner.

- **Social Cognition:** The brain is wired for social interactions, and self-development is closely tied to understanding oneself in the context of social relationships. Areas like the mirror neuron system contribute to empathy, understanding others, and developing social skills.

- **Habit Formation:** The basal ganglia and other brain regions are involved in habit formation. Positive habits contribute to self-development by fostering discipline, consistency, and personal growth over time.

- **Mindfulness & Reflection:** The brain's default mode network is associated with self-reflection and introspection. Practices like mindfulness and meditation can influence the brain's activity, promoting self-awareness and fostering personal development.

- **Neurotransmitters & Mood:** Neurotransmitters, such as serotonin and dopamine, influence mood and motivation. Balancing these chemicals is crucial for maintaining a positive mindset, resilience, and the motivation necessary for self-improvement.

- **Critical Periods & Sensitive Periods:** The brain is more plastic and adaptable during certain critical periods in development. Understanding these periods can guide efforts in self-development, emphasizing the importance of lifelong learning and personal growth.

Our brain's intricate network of neurons, synapses, and specialized regions collaborates to support self-development. Through neuroplasticity, learning, emotional regulation, and various cognitive processes, individuals can shape their thoughts, behaviors, and emotions to enhance their overall well-being and personal growth.

Becoming a Student of Your Brain to Develop Better Habits

Certainly, building better habits involves understanding the underlying mechanisms of habit formation and implementing strategies to make positive behaviors more automatic. Here are some general tips to help you build better habits:

- **Start Small:** Begin with small, manageable changes. Gradually increase the difficulty as the habit becomes more ingrained.

- **Be Specific:** Clearly define the habit you want to develop. Instead of a vague goal like "exercise more," specify: "Go for a twenty-minute walk every morning."

- **Set Clear Goals:** Establish clear and realistic goals. Break them down into short-term and long-term objectives.

- **Create a Routine:** Associate your new habit with an existing routine. For example, if you want to develop a reading habit, do it right after breakfast every day.

- **Use Triggers:** Identify triggers or cues that will remind you to perform the habit. This could be a specific time, place, or action.

- **Track Progress:** Keep a record of your efforts. Tracking your progress can be motivating and help you stay on course.

- **Stay Consistent:** Consistency is key when forming habits. Stick to your routine, even on days when motivation is low.

- **Celebrate Small Wins:** Acknowledge and celebrate your achievements along the way. This positive reinforcement can strengthen the habit loop.

- **Remove Barriers:** Make it easy to engage in the desired behavior. If your goal is to eat healthier, keep healthy snacks readily available.

- **Get Accountability:** Share your goals with someone who can provide support and hold you accountable. This could be a friend, family member, or a mentor.

- **Learn from Setbacks:** If you encounter setbacks, view them as learning opportunities rather than failures. Analyze what went wrong and adjust your approach.

- **Visualize Success:** Imagine yourself successfully completing the habit. Visualization can enhance motivation and commitment.

Tap into Your Brain Power to Guide You for Ultimate Success

If you allow yourself to truly tap into your brain power, it will provide you with a blueprint and guide for success. Your brain is more powerful than any man-made computer on the face of this earth. Use it wisely and use it often!

ERIK SWANSON

As an Award-Winning International Keynote Speaker and 13 Time #1 Bestselling Author, Erik "Mr. Awesome" Swanson is in great demand around the world! He speaks to an average of more than one million people per year. He can be seen on Amazon Prime TV in the very popular show *SpeakUP TV*. Mr. Swanson has the honor to have been invited to speak to many universities, such as the University of California (UCSD), Cal State University, University of Southern California (USC), Grand Canyon University (GCU), and the Business and Entrepreneurial School of Harvard University.

He is also a Faculty Member of CEO Space International and is a recurring keynoter at Vistage Executive Coaching. Erik also joins the Ted Talk Family with his latest TEDx speech called, "A Dose of Awesome."

Erik got his start in the self-development world by mentoring directly under the infamous Brian Tracy. Quickly climbing to become the top trainer around the world from a group of over 250 hand-picked trainers, Erik started to surround himself with the best of the best and soon started to be invited to speak on stages alongside such greats as Jim Rohn, Bob Proctor, Les Brown, Sharon Lechter, Jack Canfield, and Joe Dispenza, just to name a few.

Erik has created and developed the super-popular Habitude Warrior Conference, which has a two-year waiting list and includes thirty-three top-named speakers from around the world. It is a 'Ted Talk' style event that has quickly climbed to one of the top ten events not to miss in the United States! He is the creator, founder, and CEO of the Habitude Warrior Mastermind and Global Speakers Mastermind. His motto is clear... "NDSO!": No Drama – Serve Others!

www.SpeakerErikSwanson.com

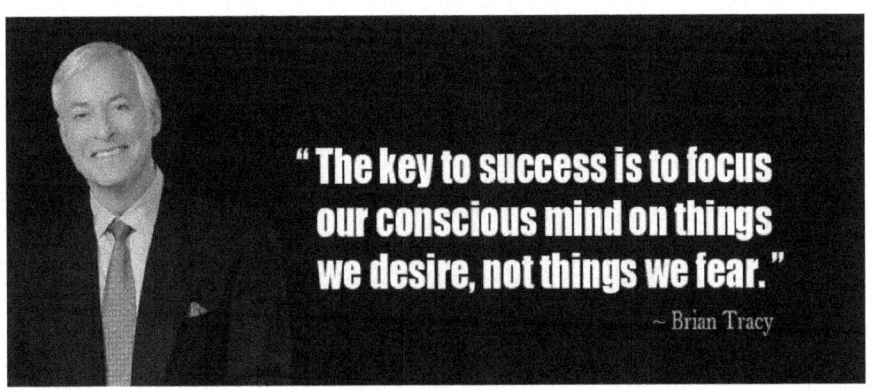

"The key to success is to focus our conscious mind on things we desire, not things we fear."

~ Brian Tracy

Jon Kovach Jr.

THE GREATEST GOD-GIVEN GIFT

Have you ever heard the phrase, "Get out of your head?" It is very likely that you've listened to it and probably said it out loud as well before. As an athlete, it's a common phrase used to instruct athletes who struggle to focus on performance instead of other circumstances; if not carefully managed, they risk being labeled as head cases.

You've probably also heard one of the phrases, "You're taking yourself too seriously," or "Lighten up." As conflicting as these phrases may be, I'm here to tell you that your head and brain can be your most incredible tool and source of power, not the root cause of any performance or achievements. Instead, it can be your greatest asset to personal growth and achievement.

When acquiring riches, your brain is the epicenter and creative conduit for all creation. Therefore, I think it's essential to give our brains more credit than they've been given before. Depending on how you have treated your brain over the years, that can be simple or complex.

Contrary to modern belief, it's better to get into your head than get out of your head. If your brain controls all energy, intelligence, and functionality, we should treat the brain with the utmost love, kindness, and respect. It's your inner-genius, high-powered engine, the master computer/controller.

Smokers willingly smoke, knowing the damage they're doing to their lungs. Alcoholics willingly drink, knowing the damage they do to their livers and kidneys. Most bad habits are still consistently committed, even with prior knowledge of their potential benefits/consequences. Now, I'm not saying people with a substance use disorder choose to be addicted; I know there are chemical and biological reactions at work. But your brain still plays a significant role in controlling those habits.

Every master controller has an off-switch, a cheat code, and a way to limit or stop various responses and reactions. People suffering from obesity issues continue to consume fatty foods, even though they know it's the number one cause of heart disease and death. And the average person, knowing that they need to feed their brain with positive, good habits and energy, continues to waste away in front of computer screens, T.V. sitcoms, phones, and nonsense entertainment.

From a fundamental perspective, we all know that reading a book, taking a walk outside, eating better, and exercising regularly are better choices than the bad habits we willingly commit periodically. Why is that?

Believe in Yourself

Our brain is the Holy Grail of energy, spark, frequency, stimulation, and signals. It is where ideas and inspiration originate. I watched a documentary of an up-and-coming snowboarder, *The Crash Reel*, about Kevin Pearce, who was a champion snowboarder and potential Olympian until a serious fall during training in 2009 left him hospitalized, suffering from a traumatic brain injury. If given a chance, Kevin could've grown his career to be greater than the G.O.A.T. of snowboarding, Shaun White.

The aftermath of just one injury, a brutal crash on a half pipe, destroyed his brain, functionalities, motor skills, and his whole life. It only took one nasty fall and blow to the head. He lives the life of a paraplegic now. The damage done to the brain could not be reversed or healed. Although, miraculously, some attempts at physical therapy and motor skill rehabilitation have allowed Kevin more opportunities than his crippled self had before, such as being able to move his feet and fingers, have full conversations, and heroically be able to live on his own again. But he would never be the same snowboarder he once was.

With that said, if the brain is the storehouse of all energy, your head is the

50

vessel and temple in which your greatest asset resides. Our bodies are the shield, shell, and surfaces of our core and soul. That also means our brain and organs are the motor, engine, and master command centers for our bodies. Also, that means that anything we choose to do with our brains and bodies and what we allow to enter our bodies are the fuel and power sources.

For example, you would NEVER put diesel in a brand new $100k sports car. Similarly, you wouldn't put anything else but the proper fuel into that vehicle other than what makes it run like a $100k sports car. We, too, should care for our life vessels (a.k.a. bodies) like a sports car.

I once met a public speaker who expressed their frustration and fear of speaking, saying that they would get performance anxiety and get all in their head negatively before their speech, leading to self-sabotage on stage. I asked them why they thought they were in control of their thoughts so much—their response was shocking. They said they couldn't face the fears of what might happen if people didn't like them on stage. I replied with the questions, "Why do you believe that there are inner thoughts you can't control? Aren't you the only person in your head?"

They were mind-blown by my inquiry, as I was merely suggesting and implying by my questions that the only person in their head is themself and that they are solely responsible for their habits, thoughts, and control. They then realized I had caught them in deceiving themself (self-deception). With one question, they realized they had been holding on to a particular belief system and forgot how to offload that belief.

Beliefs are equal to downloads. If you can subscribe to a belief, you can download a thought, just like they learn complex skills and knowledge in the movie *The Matrix*. Boom! Just like that, if you accept kung fu as a belief that something is possible, you now download the subscription that you can learn kung fu. On the contrary, if you believe that consuming alcohol will erase your pain, you will equally download that belief system despite knowing that alcohol is harmful to your body and has zero nutritional benefits.

If it's learnable, it's programmable. Convincing the brain that certain things are difficult or impossible tasks will make those things difficult and impossible. Equally, if you believe something is possible and achievable, it is now a possibility and something you can choose to pursue. The body responds to the brain. If your brain decides something is impossible, your body will equally respond. If your brain decides something is possible, your body changes its potential results. If it's learnable, then it's programmable.

The Laws of Nature

Our bodies are incredibly reactive to not only our brains but also our environments. You can fake, manipulate, and even train your brain to believe in things that were not currently possible or achieved, and your body will respond. Napoleon Hill said, "Anything you can perceive, you can achieve." If the body is merely the responder to the brain's beliefs, you can convince the body to naturally respond to things that have not yet been achieved. Remember, the brain is the master controller, and your body is its vessel.

You can train your brain and body to feel feelings and believe things into existence through the law of attraction. This is how miracles happen. This is how the impossible becomes possible. The law of attraction is the belief that positive thoughts and feelings can attract positive outcomes into your life. By focusing on the things that you want and believing that they are possible, you can begin to manifest them into reality.

This process involves a combination of visualization, positive affirmations, and gratitude. By visualizing yourself achieving your goals, telling yourself positive things, and expressing gratitude for what you already have, you can begin to shift your mindset and attract the things that you desire. By practicing the law of attraction consistently, you can train your brain and body to believe that anything is possible. With hard work and determination, you can turn your dreams into reality and create the life that you want to live.

On the contrary, the difference between believing things into existence and cognitive dissonance is that of the laws of nature. Believing things into existence is a concept that is often associated with the power of positive thinking and manifestation, which is a crucial part in the law of attraction. This idea suggests that if you believe strongly enough in something, it will come into existence or become a reality.

Cognitive dissonance, on the other hand, is a psychological term that refers to the mental discomfort experienced when holding two or more conflicting beliefs or values. While believing things into existence may work for a lot of positive people in certain situations, it is not a scientifically proven method. Cognitive dissonance is a natural and common occurrence in human beings, and it is often resolved through a process of rationalization or changing one's beliefs to match their actions.

Ultimately, the laws of nature dictate what can and cannot be brought into existence, and it is important to approach any beliefs or ideas with a critical and rational mindset.

Too many people access these natural laws of positive success but take the path of confirmation bias instead of the laws and methods that scientifically proven cognitive dissonance suggests, ultimately leading people down a path of confusion. So close to success, yet driven off course because of the wrong self-beliefs. It is important to recognize the power of our thoughts and beliefs in shaping our reality. If we hold onto limiting beliefs or biases, we may inadvertently block ourselves from achieving our goals and experiencing positive outcomes.

By embracing the natural laws of positive success and the scientifically proven methods of cognitive dissonance, we can shift our mindset and open ourselves up to new possibilities and opportunities. It takes courage and commitment to challenge our own beliefs and biases, but the rewards of doing so can be life-changing. By staying true to the path of self-improvement and growth, we can become the best versions of ourselves and achieve the success we desire.

Neuroscience

Neuroscience offers profound insights into how our brains shape our realities and dictate our potential for success. The concept of "brain plasticity" or "neuroplasticity" reveals that our brains are not static but are continuously being reshaped by our experiences and thoughts. This aligns with the foundational premise of your chapter, emphasizing that through deliberate mental exercises and positive thinking, we can rewire our brains to overcome limitations and enhance our capabilities.

For instance, research by Dr. Carol Dweck in her book *Mindset*, which focuses on the "growth mindset," underscores the transformative power of believing in our ability to grow, showing that individuals who embrace the possibility of change and development are more likely to achieve their goals and overcome challenges.

Philosophically, the Stoics believed in the power of the mind to overcome adversity and shape one's destiny. Marcus Aurelius, in his meditations, emphasized that our reactions to external events are within our control, and by mastering our thoughts, we can maintain tranquility and resilience in the face of life's challenges. This ancient wisdom echoes through your chapter's emphasis on harnessing the brain's power, suggesting that the key to riches and success lies not in external circumstances but in the disciplined management of our thoughts and perceptions.

Mind Takeovers

In reality, we are the only people with access to our brains. We are not born into mind control. Nobody else has access to your brain. Nobody has the codes, keys, or passwords to access your brain. Nobody has hijacked your brain and body. If you believe that, then you believe you are ALWAYS in control.

The most enormous facade that many still believe is that "the devil made me do it." Now you see the epiphany my client had when he realized he had a belief that there were demons in control of his brain, causing him to self-sabotage. His own doing programmed that belief, and his body was merely acting in accordance with that downloaded belief.

Remember this: Even if you are under hypnosis or any other form of mind and body takeover, nobody has FULL access to controlling you. You are always in control. If takeover controls were possible and existed today, we would have been conquered by savage, evil conquerors a long time ago already, as worldwide control is usually the desire of most villains. The reason we haven't is that it cannot be done thoroughly. But when you believe mind control by others is possible, your body responds to that download and allows takeovers to happen to the percentage capacity you allow.

One of God's greatest gifts is personal agency (the gift of individual choice). If you omit that by choice, you willingly hand over the controls to someone else. Even then, A does not equal B or C (A $\neq$ B or C). Mind control does not mean they have complete control because the body responds to the brain's beliefs. If someone believes outside-the-brain forces control them, the brain doesn't give up control; it just downloads that as belief and responds accordingly. The brain still sends signals to the body to act accordingly, which means the brain is STILL in control.

Beliefs Are Downloads

Some would claim that psychologists, therapists, and those trained in neurolinguistic programming can tap into other people's brains, but I'm afraid I have to disagree. No criminal, psychopath, or leader has access to complete 100% control over the cognitive abilities of other people.

Even to some degree, hypnosis works under the submissiveness and willingness of one person who complies with another entity, taking driving control of the mind. Under hypnosis, individuals can still think, process, act, and choose. Even at full consent, at any point in time under hypnosis, someone can break out of it, act differently, or choose not to fulfill requests.

Many people have described hypnotherapy as someone else fixing their issues, but ultimately, this is also incorrect. Hypnosis is a great way to clear someone's head so that other conflicting beliefs and programming can be moved out of the way of different beliefs to achieve results. It can be an effective form of achieving. Still, total mind control by others is impossible because the brain is the epicenter of activity and choice, and your body responds to that download.

The best experiences and results under hypnosis are when you fully submit to its process and go along with it—your brain is still the reason your body moves. It does anything that the person who put you under hypnosis requests, commands, or instructions. Like any comedy show, circus act, or excellent presentation, the presentation is only as good as its audience if you are willing to let it be.

Acceptance is Openness

For example, a famous film was released when I was in high school, *Napoleon Dynamite*. I went to the movie theater and paid to see this movie. I was shocked that everyone I knew who saw the movie thought it was "hilarious." My initial reaction to this film was that it was so stupid. I didn't get it. I even tried to get my money back. After explaining to my friends that I was not too fond of the film, they encouraged me to see it again. They said, "The first time is weird, but you'll start getting it when you see it again."

Submitting their recommendation, I reluctantly went to the theaters and paid to see the movie again. Seeing the film a second time somehow flipped a switch in my mind, and all of a sudden, *Napoleon Dynamite* was no longer a stupid film but a "hilarious" and "brilliant" movie. Nothing changed about the movie. It was and has always been the same movie, but every time I watch it, even many years later, it's still hilarious. My opinion became a belief download, and my body responded accordingly by laughing literally out loud.

Reflect

I firmly believe that "getting inside our heads" and facing ourselves and our fears in moments of solitude, silence, and even darkness are some of the most therapeutic times. You can exchange the belief of self-sabotage with the belief of unbeatable success. Like a car slipping out of control on slick roads, rather than turning away from the direction you are sliding, it is recommended you steer the wheels in the exact direction you are slipping, leaning into the source, so that you can ultimately gain full control back and straighten out the vehicle. Face yourself, your fears, and your areas of misalignment so that you can course-correct and get back on track to your success.

During these moments, we have the opportunity to reflect on our thoughts, emotions, and behaviors. We can identify patterns that are holding us back and replace them with positive affirmations and beliefs. By doing so, we can begin to shift our mindset from one of self-sabotage to one of unbeatable success. It's important to remember that this process takes time and patience, but the rewards are truly life-changing. Embrace the darkness and use it as a tool to unlock your full potential.

Achieving Through Activity

Recent advancements in neuroscience have illuminated the incredible plasticity of the human brain, a concept that fundamentally alters our understanding of personal growth and achievement. Studies, such as those conducted by neuroscientist Dr. Michael Merzenich, demonstrate that engaging in new, challenging activities can significantly enhance cognitive abilities by forging new neural pathways. This neuroplasticity, the brain's ability to reorganize itself by forming new neural connections throughout life, serves as the scientific backbone of our discussion. It underscores the potential within each of us to reshape our brains and, by extension, our capabilities and destinies through deliberate practice and thought patterns.

Nurture Through Brain-er-cises

One of my favorite recreational activities to do is swimming. I love it because I can literally plug my ears, plug my nose, close my eyes, and submerge under water. Underwater, all you can hear is the ringing sound of silence. Similarly, I love living in the mountains where I don't have the perpetual noise of traffic and generators. Instead, I can access pure silence and nature, the sound of nothing. These moments allow me to be present and focus on my inner thoughts.

When you position your thoughts against a pinned, inescapable physical experience, you can learn much about your ability and what's wrong. There's nothing wrong with it; you need to grow a different perspective and allow it to blossom so that you can have greater peace and fulfillment.

The brain is the epicenter of all success, and I often wonder what's happening in other people's brains. It's my favorite activity to sit in public places and watch people as I observe as a bystander and see people act, their behaviors, what they say, and what they do. It sounds creepy, but we call it people-watching for a reason, and it's addictive and fun. To observe many people go through daily life just like you do and behave and act differently is a fascinating experience and experiment. No harm done, no judgment, just observation.

Sit, watch, and listen! This activity is renowned for helping you focus solely on one task and item. I encourage you to be willing to submit to such a process where you will develop a continuous and ongoing relationship and conversation with yourself and strengthen your inner intuition. Like an old friend where you can pick up right where you left off, you must rely on yourself and your abilities to get clear with your realities.

As you observe others, take note of what draws your attention and what you find interesting. Perhaps it's someone's outfit, their body language, or the way they interact with others. Use these observations to gain insight into your own preferences and tendencies. Additionally, people-watching can teach us about empathy and understanding.

When we observe others going through their daily lives, we can begin to understand the challenges and joys that they face. It's a reminder that we all have our own unique experiences and perspectives. So the next time you find yourself with a bit of free time, grab a seat in a public place and start people-watching. You never know what you might learn about yourself and the world around you.

Practical Exercise—Envisioning Activity

To tap into the potential of your brain and instigate change, I recommend the "5-Minute Envisionment Training" exercise, a methodology shared in my excerpts in volumes 3 (Auto-Suggestion) and 10 (Transmutation).

Each morning, dedicate five minutes to close your eyes and vividly imagine achieving one of your goals. Engage all your senses in this visualization. What do you see? How do you feel? What sounds surround you as you achieve this success? This exercise not only primes your brain to recognize and seize opportunities that align with your goals but also enhances your neuroplasticity, making it a powerful tool for personal transformation.

One common challenge in harnessing the power of the brain is overcoming ingrained negative thought patterns, which can be a significant barrier to personal growth. A practical solution to this challenge is the practice of "Cognitive Restructuring," a cognitive-behavioral therapy technique.

Whenever you catch yourself engaged in negative self-talk, actively challenge and replace these thoughts with positive affirmations. For instance, replace thoughts of "I can't do this" with "I am capable and prepared to tackle this challenge." This not only helps in rewiring your brain for positivity but also in building a resilient mindset conducive to achieving your aspirations.

Advanced Mindfulness Techniques

Incorporating advanced mindfulness techniques such as "Focused Attention Meditation" and "Open Monitoring Meditation" can significantly enhance cognitive flexibility and emotional regulation. Focused Attention Meditation involves concentrating on a single object, breath, or thought, training the brain to maintain focus and resist distractions. Open Monitoring Meditation, on the other hand, encourages a broad awareness of all aspects of the environment, thoughts, and sensations without attachment.

These practices not only improve attention and clarity of thought but also foster a deeper connection to one's inner wisdom and creative potential, aligning with the chapter's message of unlocking the brain's power.

Some of the world's most talented and top athletes experience a deep sense of focus where they can vividly remember every aspect of the game or performance, but never remember or recall the sounds of the audience or those cheering from the bleachers. Their ability to focus solely on "the game" or "performance" magically turns off their peripheral awareness, which can lead to thoughts of distraction.

This state of deep focus is commonly referred to as being "in the zone" or experiencing "flow." It is a mental state where one is completely absorbed in the task at hand, and distractions seem to fade away. Athletes who experience this state often report feeling a sense of timelessness, as if time is standing still and they are completely in the present moment.

Interestingly, this state of flow is associated not just with athletes but with individuals in a wide range of fields, from artists to scientists and even musicians. It is a state of mind that allows one to tap into their very best performances. While the state of flow may seem elusive, there are techniques that one can use to cultivate it. These include focusing on the present moment, setting clear goals, and breaking down tasks into manageable chunks. With practice and persistence, anyone can tap into the power of flow, and achieve their full potential in whatever field they choose.

Cutting-edge Technology Resources

Several accessible technologies offer exciting possibilities for enhancing brain function and achieving personal growth. Modern-day apps and resources available to the public, like "Headspace" and "Calm," provide guided meditations that can improve mindfulness and reduce stress, while devices such as the "Muse" headband offer real-time feedback on your meditation practice by monitoring brain activity.

Furthermore, platforms like "Lumosity" and "Peak" offer brain-training games designed to improve cognitive functions such as memory, attention, and problem-solving skills. These resources democratize access to brain enhancement techniques, empowering individuals to take charge of their mental fitness and, by extension, their path to success.

In addition to these helpful resources, I recently discovered a song called "Weightless" by Marconi Union, which was said to help calm the mind and reduce stress by significant percentages in listeners. The song "Weightless" was acknowledged by Time Magazine, which included Marconi Union on their list of Inventors of the Year in 2011.

"Weightless" is incredibly effective in reducing stress levels, making it a go-to for those looking for ways to calm their minds. The song has a slow and steady rhythm that is designed to ease listeners into a state of relaxation and meditation. Sharing from personal experience, their music has had a significant impact on the way people approach stress management. I recommend you give it a go.

On my podcast, *Circle of Knowledge,* I offer a free meditative resource called "Champion Mindset Training," which takes you through a six to eight-minute breathing and envisionment exercise I've used to help elite athletes and high-performing professionals achieve their goals and overcome mind blocks. It's free and available to the public. Just visit the *Circle of Knowledge* podcast on Spotify and search for the episode titled "Champion Mindset Training" for full unlimited access.

Meditation has been proven to have many benefits, including reducing stress and anxiety, improving focus and concentration, and promoting better sleep. The Champion Mindset Training exercise combines meditation with visualization, helping individuals focus their minds on achieving their goals. By practicing this exercise regularly, you can train your mind to overcome obstacles and stay focused on your objectives. Whether you're an athlete looking to improve your performance or a professional striving to reach your full potential, this exercise can help you unlock your inner champion.

Mastering the Master Mind: The Keystone of Achieving Riches

Out of all the technologies, apps, resources, and methodologies out there, there is one that I have found to be far more superior and effective than them all, which is the Mastermind. Napoleon Hill's concept of the Master Mind group is perhaps one of the most transformative methodologies in the pursuit of success and personal growth. At its core, a Mastermind group is a collective of individuals dedicated to mutual improvement, sharing a common goal of achieving personal and professional growth.

Hill defined the Mastermind as a "coordination of knowledge and effort, in a spirit of harmony, between two or more people, for the attainment of a definite purpose." This principle is not just a strategy but a profound exercise in utilizing the brain's utmost capabilities—our most vital organ and muscle—toward achieving unparalleled success.

The power of a Mastermind group lies in its ability to harness the diverse experiences, skills, and insights of its members, creating a synergistic effect that surpasses the sum of its parts. It's an ultimate brain exercise, pushing each member to think creatively, solve problems collaboratively, and expand their cognitive boundaries beyond individual limits. This collaborative environment fosters a unique space for sharing challenges, brainstorming solutions, and holding one another accountable to the highest standards of personal and professional excellence.

As a Global Mastermind Leader, I have witnessed firsthand the transformative power of well-structured Mastermind groups. My personal journey and success are testaments to the efficacy of this methodology. Dedicating my life and career to teaching and educating professionals about Mastermind methodologies has not only been my passion but also my greatest tool for achieving accelerated results and success. The collective brainpower of a Mastermind group can illuminate paths that were once hidden, uncover solutions that seemed elusive, and propel its members toward their goals at an astonishing pace.

In my experience, the most successful Mastermind groups operate on principles of trust, respect, and confidentiality, creating a safe space for vulnerability and genuine sharing. Each member brings their unique strengths and perspectives to the table, enriching the group's collective wisdom. As we navigate through the complexities of our professional and personal lives, the Mastermind serves as a lighthouse, guiding us through uncharted waters with the collective insights and support of its members.

The ultimate exercise of participating in a Mastermind group lies not just in the sharing of knowledge and resources but in the profound personal transformation that occurs. Members often experience significant shifts in their mindset, adopting a more expansive, abundance-oriented approach to life and work. This mindset shift is the crux of tapping into the brain's latent potential, turning obstacles into opportunities, and transforming dreams into tangible achievements.

The Mastermind principle is not merely a methodology for success; it's a way of life. It embodies the essence of collaborative intelligence and the incredible power of the human brain when aligned with others in harmony and purpose. As we continue to explore the depths of our minds and the boundless possibilities they hold, let us remember that together, we can achieve far more than we ever could alone. The Mastermind, therefore, stands as a beacon of collective achievement and personal mastery, a testament to the indomitable power of the human spirit and intellect.

Embrace the boundless potential that resides within the corridors of your mind. Let this chapter serve as a beacon, guiding you toward a journey of self-discovery and unparalleled achievement. I invite you to step beyond the confines of doubt and harness the incredible power of your brain. Together, let's embark on this transformative path, where the only limits that exist are those we place upon ourselves.

Remember, the greatest achievements begin with a single thought, a spark within the vastness of your mind. Let that spark ignite into a flame of passion, purpose, and prosperity. Join me in this quest for excellence, and let us unlock the doors to a future brimming with riches beyond measure.

JON KOVACH JR

About Jon Kovach Jr.: Jon is an award-winning international motivational speaker and global mastermind leader. Jon has helped multi-billion-dollar corporations exceed their annual sales goals, including Coldwell Banker Commercial, outdoor retailer Cotopaxi, and the Public Relations Student Society of America. In addition, in his work as an accountability coach and mastermind facilitator, Jon has helped thousands of professionals overcome their challenges and achieve their goals by implementing his accountability strategies and Irrefutable Laws of High Performance. Jon is the Founder and Chairman of Champion Circle, a professional development association that combines high-performance-based networking activities and recreational fun to create connection capital and increase prosperity for professionals. Jon is the Mastermind Facilitator and Team Lead of the Habitude Warrior Mastermind and the Global Speakers Mastermind & Masterclass founded by Speaker Erik "Mr. Awesome" Swanson.

Jon speaks on topics including accountability, his Irrefutable Laws of High Performance, and The Power of Mastermind Methodologies. He is a #1 Bestselling Author and a featured keynote on *SpeakUp TV*, an Amazon Prime TV series, with his keynote speech titled, *Getting Unstuck*. In addition, he stars in over 100 speaking stages, podcasts, and live international summits each year. Jon's motivational messages have been viewed by over 500,000 people online. His positive messages have trended and been used by global brands on TikTok and Instagram, such as: Red Bull, Michael Bublé, NHL, Powell Books, GoDaddy Studio, Canada's Wonderland Amusement Park, and the LSU Cheer Team.

Author's Website: *www.JonKovachJr.com*

Book Series Website: *www.The13StepsToRiches.com*

Amado Hernandez

IF YOU ONLY HAD A BRAIN

DEDICATED TO MY CHILDREN:
Roberto, Ricardo, Joshua, and Stacy Sarah
AND MY GRANDCHILDREN
Robbie in Heaven
Olivia Grace, Caleb, Isaiah, Marc Joshua, Annabelle,
Sophia, Ava, and Mila

"My brain, I believe, is the most beautiful part of my body."
~ Shakira

Thirty-seven years before Napoleon Hill published *Think and Grow Rich*, Dorothy Gale encountered a living scarecrow in a field in Munchkin Country. Dorothy and her little dog, Toto, had been swept away to the Land of Oz by a tornado. Dorothy and Toto were on their way to the Emerald City to ask the Wizard of Oz to help them return home. The "mindless" scarecrow joined Dorothy and Toto, hoping that the Wizard would give him a brain.

Most of us have watched the encounter between Dorothy and the Scarecrow in Metro-Goldwyn-Mayer's fantasy film released two years after *Think and Grow Rich* hit the bookshelves in 1937. Here are the lyrics to their legendarily adorable musical exchange:

Dorothy: "What would you do with a brain if you had one?"

Scarecrow: "Do? Why, if I had a brain, I could—I could while away the hours conferrin' with the flowers—consultin' with the rain. And

65

my head I'd be scratchin' while my thoughts were busy hatchin' if I only had a brain. I'd unravel every riddle for any individual in trouble or in pain."

Dorothy: "With the thoughts, you'll be thinkin', you could be another Lincoln if you only had a brain."

Scarecrow: "Oh, I could tell you why the ocean's near the shore. I could think of things I never thunk before. And then I'd sit and think some more. I would not be just a nothin', my head all full of stuffin'—my heart all full of pain. I would dance and be merry—life would be a ding-a-derry if I only had a brain."

L. Frank Baum's comical and iconic scarecrow appeared throughout the Oz books and movies. *The Wonderful Wizard of Oz* has been interpreted by many economists, historians, and political scientists as a political allegory portraying the Scarecrow as the popular impression of the American farmer. There was a time when some farmers were viewed as "stupid hicks" even though they possessed common sense, logic, and quick wit. The underlying message and theme in all the Oz works is that everyone possesses the resources they need to succeed (such as a brain, a heart, and courage) if only they had *self-confidence.*

And that brings us back to Napoleon Hill. Isn't that the underlying message and common theme throughout *Think and Grow Rich?* In the final analysis, God has given us everything we need to be "healthy, wealthy, and wise" (the broad meaning of *rich*)—and even be "happy." The lessons of *Think and Grow Rich* were designed to give us the *self-*confidence we need from *Desire* to *Clearing the Brain for Riches (How to Outwit the Six Ghosts of Fear).*

Imagine yourself for a moment, an hour—or even a day—as a mindless scarecrow with a head stuffed with straw. And maybe even imagine that your head is being attacked by a bunch of crows. In our current *permacrisis,* many of us might feel pretty much like that on any given day. And we might even feel that we might be better off as a brainless "stupid hick" possessing common sense, logic, and quick wit instead of having the IQ of a Mensa member.

Our brains can be our best friends—or our worst enemies. They can create dreams—and they can create nightmares. They can make us happy —and they can make us miserable. With the priceless gift of our brains that God gave us comes both opportunity as well as responsibility. While each of us can create our own individual "opportunities," we all have universal responsibilities to our brains that begin the moment that we realize that we have one (a brain).

The first responsibility that we have is to *protect our brain from injuries.* The best example of this is wearing a helmet when we ride a bicycle or participate in what might be considered a more *dangerous* activity (i.e., boxing, skydiving, auto racing, bungee jumping, ziplining—all the fun stuff). Kids need to protect their brains with helmets while skateboarding or riding a scooter and especially speeding on those now-popular electric bikes.

The second responsibility we have is to *protect our brain from damage.* Brain damage can come from diseases, prescription and recreational drugs, alcohol, smoking, and the ingestion or exposure to toxic chemicals and substances. It may even come from the consumption of contaminated foods and beverages, high fevers, and prolonged exposure to extreme temperatures.

The third responsibility we have is to *nourish, hydrate, and oxygenate* our brains through proper nutrition, liquids, and aerobic exercise. By taking care of our bodies, we also take care of our organs—including our brain.

The fourth responsibility that we have is to *exercise* our brains. We can exercise our brains in many ways—from computer games to sports to crossword puzzles and anything and everything that challenges the status quo of a "lazy" brain. Create a training or workout schedule to exercise your brain the same way you would be expected to do for physical exercise.

The fifth responsibility that we have is to *use* our brains as much as possible—to challenge our brains and push toward their limitless powers of imagination, vision, creativity, and mega-performance.

The sixth—and final—responsibility we have is to *rest* our brains through sleep and relaxation. This includes meditation, grounding, and *especially* disconnecting from the social media grid for significant amounts of time.

This chapter is dedicated to my children and grandchildren—and their children and grandchildren for one simple reason. My primary legacy to my family—the wisdom that I want to leave them—is in the words of these simple sentences: *Thank God for your brain. It is the only one you'll ever have. Cherish it. Protect it. Nourish it. Exercise it. And, most importantly, constantly fill it with fresh, positive, empowering thoughts. Guard your brain against negative self-talk and the words, thoughts, and actions of toxic people.*

Think back to when you were a kid. None of us really remember when we realized that we had a brain. Maybe in kindergarten or in sixth-grade science class or tenth-grade biology. But our brains started working before we were born. A popular belief is that electrical activity starts around eight weeks after pregnancy begins.

Remember when you first tried to stand up on your own and walk? Every time you fell down, your brain told you to stand back up and try again to walk. It happened again and again and again—until, finally, you "learned" to walk. No one "taught" you to walk. It was all about God, your brain, and you.

But what happened along the way? Eventually, you discover that you might get hurt by falling. So, every fall conditioned you to be more "cautious," and your experiences programmed your mind. That's a good thing—and a bad thing. While it's usually good to be careful, sometimes it's counter-productive to growth and development.

So, my final message to my children and grandchildren? Reach for the stars, but try to always keep at least one foot on the ground. Be careful but take *calculated risks* along life's journey to ensure that you experience as much of the thing that we call *"life"* as possible. As we get older, many of us look back at our lives and think to ourselves: "I wish I would have done more." In the words of the "Great One," Wayne Gretzky: "You miss 100% of the shots you don't take."

Develop your brain power and take advantage of it to solve problems, create dreams, accomplish great things, and live the life you deserve to live. Change lives and make your world a better place. You don't need to travel to *The Land of Oz*. God has blessed you with a brain, a heart, and courage. You're the Scarecrow, Tin Man, and Lion all rolled into one unique, amazing, self-confident, beautiful person.

Remember those early computer terms like "WYSIWYG" (What You See is What You Get) and "Trash in, Trash out"? Pure and simple, that's how our brains function. Guard, with a vengeance, what you *allow* into your brain—and more critically—filter (censor) what your brain tells you and what your brain tells you to tell other people. Let your brain do "the heavy lifting" for you. And program your brain to *think and grow rich now.*

AMADO HERNANDEZ

About Amado Hernandez: Amado was born in Mexico of humble beginnings and raised in Los Angeles, California. As an avid reader, Amado always focused on self-development. He coaches sales professionals to make six and seven figures in real estate.

Amado believes in a progressive culture, a people-centric culture where clients' dreams come true, and salespeople thrive; at the end of the day, we all want to be respected and pursue our happiness. My goal is to leave a legacy-making a difference in people's lives.

With thirty-three years of Real Estate experience, Mr. ABC Amado Hernandez successfully operates and grows his Excellence Empire Real Estate Moreno Valley office. Broker/Owner Amado first opened his doors in 1995, and Excellence currently has over sixty offices in Southern California, Las Vegas, Merida Yucatan, Mexico, and over 1,000 Agents.

He is also part owner of a highly successful Mortgage company, Excellence Mortgage, and owner of Empire Escrow Services. Mr. Amado is also involved with his community and currently serves as Director at Inland Valley Association of Realtors and will be the President-Elect for 2023. Amado serves as a Director of CAR (California Association of Realtors).

Author's Website: *www.ExcellenceEmpireRE.com*

Book Series Website: *www.The13StepsToRiches.com*

Angelika Ullsperger

UNLEASHING YOUR GREATEST POWER

"If the brain were so simple that we could understand it, we would be so simple, we couldn't."
~ **Emerson Pugh**

How are you reading this sentence? With your eyes, yes, but how do you know what you're seeing, and more importantly, how are you able to comprehend what these symbols even mean? For centuries people have pondered over the question: "How does the brain actually work?" It's a miracle that we are able to see, hear, taste, and touch, yet philosophers and scientists alike have been baffled by the inner workings of the human brain.

The brain is arguably the most essential part of the body. While the heart, lungs, and other organs are necessary for life, the brain is required for consciousness, and it is our consciousness that shapes our entire reality. But what if I told you, you're not stuck with the brain you have? You can always work on changing your brain, and contrary to popular belief, an old dog CAN learn new tricks. We can use these tricks to fuel us towards success.

The second you're born, you have all the neurons you will ever have. It's the connections between these cells that make the brain work, and these connections will shape our development. One of the significant ways these connections form is through our caretakers and how they talk to us.

If we are spoken to with compassion, we will begin to develop an inner voice that is understanding, whereas if we are treated harshly, we will learn to treat ourselves poorly. Sometimes, your brain will tell you things that aren't true. It might try to knock you down, but remember, you are not your thoughts; you are the consciousness behind them. It's hard to be a kid and have no knowledge of how your brain is being shaped. It's a heavy realization, but this knowledge opens your mind to change and empowers us to reshape our brains. In the past, I have felt so powerless but the realization I can recondition my brain gave me the strength I needed to keep going.

Growing up, there were too many times trauma shaped my life. I'm blessed to say although divorced, I have two wonderful parents who love me very much. Yet, in some ways, I grew up in a chaotic environment. I experienced many traumas from childhood into adulthood. It was all of these back-to-back traumas that negatively shaped my brain and my inner thoughts. For a long time, I thought I was stuck. held down by the immense weight of sadness, I felt ashamed and worthless. Wanting to at least understand why I was acting this way, I began reading in depth about psychology. I did not know it at the time, but what I would learn would save me from the life I once knew.

Everyone goes through something in high school, and I went through a lot of "somethings," to say the least. One of the biggest obstacles was my first serious relationship. It wasn't like the typical cute, innocent high school crush. It began because I was assaulted by someone who I thought was a friend. I would often dissociate to escape, which led me into a relationship with the person. At the time, being with this person was the escape from the toxic environment I was stuck in, and although I know it wasn't a good choice, at the time it was the lesser of two bad situations. I fought with depression so hard, suffering in the environment I was stuck in and for a brief moment, I overcame it.

Even after getting temporarily stuck in an abusive relationship, I was making progress. Being in a depressive state had taken a toll on my motivation and was reflected in my schoolwork. Then, after barely graduating high school, I lost both of my grandparents. The people who took care of me growing up were gone. My mom at the time was dealing with her own traumas, and I almost lost her during that time as well. When I thought things couldn't get worse, the unthinkable happened.

Nothing could have prepared me for what was coming next. My mother was dating a man by the name of Scott, who was like a second dad to me. Scott, however, struggled with his own battles. One day, Scott was really struggling, so I made the difficult choice to call 911. They shot him and left him to bleed out for hours. It was that experience that left me destroyed. I never expected a call for help to go so wrong so fast.

After getting through so many immensely difficult situations, this broke me back down. The brain is fueled by inputs and because so many negative events were put into my brain, it negatively affected how my brain worked and how I functioned. That experience traumatized me for some time, yet it is the knowledge I can change my brain that keeps me going. Knowing that as long as I keep trying I will continue to heal. it is only a matter of time before things improve.

In the vast landscape of the human mind, the journey to success begins with understanding the intricate workings of the brain. *Think and Grow Rich* came out around eighty-six years ago, and there have been monumental discoveries and advances in every walk of life since. By mixing Hill's work with exploration into the neuroscience of success, we can begin to unravel the mysteries of the brain's incredible potential for growth and adaptation.

Contrary to the once-held belief that the brain's structure is fixed, neuroplasticity reveals the brain's remarkable ability to reorganize itself. This phenomenon occurs in response to learning, experience, and intentional mental exercises. And it is this very phenomenon that allowed me to change my brain to change my life.

No one is stuck. Is it about learning the information we need to move forward? I learned most of mine through trial and error, so hopefully, by sharing what allowed me to change, you can avoid some of the same problems I've experienced.

Of course, there are the basics we've all heard: drink water, get enough sleep, and get exercise. Many people take this for granted, not realizing the difference with or without. It's vital to be mindful and pay attention to your actions (or lack of) and the effects on everything from how you feel to how you think. Even the small things can make a big difference when it comes to brain function.

The brain operates like a complex network of interconnected circuits. The better we understand their interactions the better we can take advantage of them. Success begins with deliberately influencing this network through the power of intention. Setting clear and well-defined goals activates specific neural pathways, aligning your thoughts and actions with the desired outcome.

If that outcome is success, then it's also important to know success thrives on clarity. Our brains work best when given clear and specific instructions. By defining your goals with precision, you provide your brain with a roadmap, guiding its neural circuits toward the desired outcome.

The prefrontal cortex, the main one in charge of executive functions, plays a pivotal role in decision-making, goal-setting, and self-control. Understanding how this region operates provides insights into how to effectively set and pursue your goals. As someone who struggles with ADHD, I have to find ways to work with my brain instead of letting it work against me.

No matter who you are, your brain is going to work slightly differently due to an amalgamation of many things, including circumstances, events, and genetics. We are all valid, but we must also consider that we will have to tailor strategies to work with who we are.

So much time has passed since T&GR. Thanks to advances in technology, many new schools of thought, ideologies, and discoveries have come about. It is these changes that allow us to optimize our brains even further. Sometimes, I find Cognitive Behavioral Therapy and Psychitecture helpful, which are the ideas of designing and restructuring your mind.

Because we now know more about how the brain works, we can make educated choices about which habits and strategies we should test and implement.

While you can't shape your past, you can shape your environment to shape your brain, which shapes your future. Being able to take a step back and see these connections is part of what allows us to work with our brains and not against them.

Here is one of my most difficult negative chain reactions:

If I'm feeling sad, I'll take a nap, which is totally fine, as sleep is beneficial to one's cognitive function. The problem arises when I begin to get stuck in a cycle of oversleeping to the point I am more tired. As you guessed it, this makes me sleep even more, which makes me become depressed. As a result of not having the energy and sleeping so much, I don't get anything accomplished, which makes me more stressed and depressed.

If I don't stay present and aware, this cycle continues. After this pattern repeated so much without me being able to do much against it, I 'out' myself in a different environment. An environment that pushes me to do what I need to and keeps me away from what is detrimental.

It can be hard to get things started without any dopamine, so I've learned I need to keep my momentum up. To start with something small and easy to start the momentum. I use the dopamine from accomplishing the smaller tasks to move to the bigger tasks.

Dopamine is a neurotransmitter associated with pleasure and reward, which plays a crucial role in motivation. Setting and achieving goals triggers the release of dopamine, reinforcing positive behaviors and creating a sense of satisfaction.

One thing I never liked was affirmations. To be frank, they irritated me. The idea that people could repeat things and become happy was hogwash in my eyes. I thought they hadn't been through it; it's easy for them to say that works eventually; once I realized by changing my inputs, I could change my brain, I realized words have the power to shape thoughts, beliefs, and, ultimately, actions. The way you speak to yourself shapes your self-perception and influences your actions. Positive self-talk acts as a form of self-encouragement, rewiring neural pathways to support confidence, motivation, and resilience. Affirmations, when crafted with positivity and intention, act as a form of positive programming for the brain, rewiring neural pathways to support your goals.

So, what did I begin to do? I began to develop affirmations that resonated with my goals and aspirations and repeated them regularly to embed positive messages into my subconscious mind. As you consistently reinforce positive beliefs, you lay the groundwork for a neurological blueprint that aligns seamlessly with your path to success.

In setting your neurological blueprint, clarity, visualization, prefrontal cortex engagement, dopamine release, and positive programming form the building blocks of success. By consciously shaping your goals and consistently reinforcing them, you empower your brain to navigate the intricate journey toward achievement with purpose and determination.

As you navigate the dynamic landscape of success, recognize that the strength of your neural networks shapes your cognitive abilities and behaviors. By actively engaging in activities that promote neuroplasticity and building positive habits, you lay the foundation for a resilient and adaptable brain that propels you toward your goals.

These days, due to the practices I shared above, along with others, I am doing much better. I still have off days, but that's ok. I've come to realize that not even the happiest people are happy all the time, even if they have their bad days. Happiness is a skill that can be improved upon. When I feel down, I make sure to stay extra cognizant and allocate extra time to get back into good habits. You don't deserve to give yourself a hard time for struggling. Have patience. Changing the brain takes time, but with time comes growth, and it is that growth that will change your life.

ANGELIKA ULLSPERGER

About Angelika Ullsperger: Angelika is a serial entrepreneur from Baltimore, Maryland. She is a fashion designer, model, artist, photographer, and musician. Angelika has extensive and well-rounded professional experience, having worked as a business owner, carpenter, chef, graphic designer, manager, event planner, sales and product specialist, marketer, and coach. Angelika is now a #1 Bestselling Author in the historic book series, *The 13 Steps to Riches*. She is a life-long learner with a sincere and genuine interest in all things of the world with a major interest in the formal subject of abnormal psychology, neuroscience, and quantum physics.

Angelika prides herself as someone who has saved lives as a friend, first responder, EMT, and knowledgeable suicide prevention advocate. With vast knowledge and experience in multiple professions, Angelika is also a proud, honorable member of Phi Theta Kappa, The APA, the AAAS, and an FBLA (Future Business Leaders Association) Business Competition Finalist. She is Certified in basic coding and blockchain technology. Amongst the careers and vast experience, Angelika is an adventurer and avid dog lover.

Her ultimate goals and dreams are to make a lasting positive impact in people's lives through her wealth of knowledge and skillsets.

Author's Website: *www.Angelika.world*

Book Series Website: *www.The13StepsToRiches.com*

Dr. Anthony M. Criniti IV

THE GREATEST INTANGIBLE FORCE

Think and Grow Rich by Napoleon Hill is one of the best classic books to teach someone about how to become a financial success (as well as a success in other areas of life). In there, you will find his thirteen steps to riches; each one has its own separate chapter and analysis. The subject of our book is to interpret his twelfth step to riches: The Brain. Let's review some of the major highlights of this chapter.

Chapter 13 (The Brain) is an extremely short chapter; nevertheless, it packs a powerful punch that can keep you up all night thinking about its deep conclusions. Despite the title, this chapter does not contain medical knowledge about the brain in the way that various biology textbooks would. Instead, Hill approaches the subject from an angle that many might consider to be on the edge and quasi-scientific. He builds his theories on how the brain works based on the major technology of his time: the radio.

If we use the definition of science that was stated in my first book, Hill's theories can find a home in science because it leveraged the knowledge of many of the brightest scientists of that period (who invented things that were once called "crazy" ideas). As stated in *The Necessity of Finance*: "…science is a persistent search for a truly better way to perform an action or understand a condition, process, or thing"…"That is, science allows for progressive learning, refinement of our daily thoughts, and searching for truth in order to find a truly better way to perform an action or understand a condition, process, or thing" (Criniti, 2013, p. 3-4).

Hill describes his perspective of the brain: "More than twenty years ago, the author working in conjunction with the late Dr. Alexander Graham Bell, and Dr. Elmer R. Gates, observed that every human brain is both a broadcasting and receiving station for the vibration of thought. Through the medium of the ether, in a fashion similar to that employed by the radio broadcasting principle, every human brain is capable of picking up vibrations of thought which are being released by other brains" (Hill, 2011, p. 302).

If our minds are broadcasting and receiving stations for thoughts in the way that the radio operates, there could be thoughts flying all over the air. Our minds might build mental fortresses to protect us from these "flying thoughts," which partially explains how our generation has become desensitized to the amount of ads that we are constantly bombarded with. We need these mental firewalls to protect us from intruders. After all, there are extraordinarily unethical people who can convince anyone to buy things that they don't want *without reading their minds*. As stated in Principle 89 of *The Most Important Lessons in Economics and Finance*: "It is important to beware of individuals with extraordinary influencing abilities" (Criniti, 2014, p. 121). Imagine what these people can do if they can intercept one's thoughts.

Highly unethical, influential people might not be able to read people's minds, but they sure will try. At a minimum, most of them know how to get their thoughts to break through our mental barriers and get our attention. How? Enter emotions. Hill goes on to elaborate on this process: "When stimulated, or "stepped up" to a high rate of vibration, the mind becomes more receptive to the vibration of thought which reaches it through the ether from outside sources. This "stepping up" process takes place through the positive emotions, or the negative emotions. Through the emotions, the vibrations of thought may be increased. Vibrations of an exceedingly high rate are the only vibrations picked up and carried, by the ether, from one brain to another" (Hill, 2011, p. 302-303).

Hill explains the mechanics of the similarities of the brain to radio: "Thus, you will see that the broadcasting principle is the factor through which you mix feeling, or emotion with your thoughts and pass them on to your subconscious mind. The subconscious mind is the "sending station" of the brain, through which vibrations of thought are broadcast. The Creative Imagination is the "receiving set," through which the vibrations of thought are picked up from the ether" (Hill, 2011, p. 303-304).

Another important part of this chapter worth highlighting is the experiments that Hill conducted to prove several of his theories. In particular, by using experiments with telepathy between him and his peers, he tried to prove the validity of the mastermind concept. His experiments were important because if you can demonstrate that our minds are like broadcasting and receiving stations to other minds, it can demonstrate how much more powerful a collective group of minds can be (in theory, the thinking power should expand).

Hill describes his experiment: "In view of Dr. Rhine's announcement in connection with the conditions under which the mind responds to what he terms "extra-sensory" modes of perception, I now feel privileged to add to his testimony by stating that my associates and I have discovered what we believe to be the ideal conditions under which the mind can be stimulated so that the sixth sense described in the next chapter, can be made to function in a practical way. The conditions to which I refer consist of a close working alliance between myself and two members of my staff" (Hill, 2011, p. 309).

To round up our analysis of this chapter, we come full circle to understand Hill's conclusions on the brain and its most powerful tool: the thought. As a scientist, from the first time I read Napoleon Hill many years ago, I appreciated how much of a deep thinker he was. I also liked that he was not afraid to test out his theories…even if they sounded very unusual to the masses. He is also quick to admit where humanity is deficient, for example, with our lack of knowledge of the intangibles: "Sometimes men speak lightly of the intangibles—the things which they cannot perceive through any of their five senses, and when we hear them, it should remind us that *all of us are controlled by forces which are unseen and intangible"* (Hill, 2011, p. 305).

Hill even questions the mere purpose of the brain for survival only (which was believed to be the main role by many biologists of his time): "It is inconceivable that such a network of intricate machinery should be in existence for the sole purpose of carrying on the physical functions incidental to growth and maintenance of the physical body. Is it not likely that the same system, which gives billions of brain cells the media for communication one with another, provides, also the means of communication with other intangible forces?" (Hill, 2011, p. 306).

This last question is too powerful to leave inserted in a chapter this size. However, it becomes a connecting point to his other conclusions on telepathy, and possibly, the ability for us to have a direct line of communication through our imagination with infinite intelligence.

One of the highlighting parts of this chapter for me was the specific language that Hill used to describe a *thought:* "the greatest of all the intangibles." He mentioned other intangible forces that humanity could not control and/or understand fully: the rolling waves of the ocean, gravity, a thunderstorm, electricity, and the soil of the earth. But he specifically ruled the "thought" as king of them all: "Last, but not least, man, with all of his boasted culture and education, understands little or nothing of the intangible force (the greatest of all the intangibles) of *thought.* He knows but little concerning the physical brain, and its vast network of intricate machinery through which the power of thought is translated into its material equivalent, but he is now entering an age which shall yield enlightenment on the subject" (Hill, 2011, p. 305-306).

I had a very similar conclusion to Hill in my last book published in 2016. After analyzing all of the things that humans have learned to control over time (illustrated through what I called the "General Control Scale of Nature"), I realized that humans only have two unconquered enemies from "living nature": *ourselves* and the *microscopic.* From *The Survival of the Richest:* "A significant upward trend appears to have occurred over tens of thousands of years, particularly in the past few hundred years, as humanity has gained control over nonhuman nature. For example, from the perspective of human nature versus the rest of living nature, it should be clear that the battle has been more or less won for some time now. Most remaining problems from the living parts of nature now mainly include the microscopic (bacteria and viruses) and ourselves (human warfare)" (Criniti, 2016, p. 275).

Ultimately, with more reflection, the reference to "ourselves" was really referring to control over the thoughts in our minds. Like Hill, I concluded that we know little about our own thoughts, but also foreshadowed that our minds (as well as the microscopic) were the next battlefields that we must win to gain full control over living nature.

In conclusion, perhaps, the thought is the greatest intangible force. After all, all living things in this world, and their creations, were created by a thought. But what is a thought? Where does a thought come from? Why do we have thoughts? The answers to these questions, in all probability, have something to do with the answers to the mysteries of the other intangibles forces Hill mentioned. Since our thoughts become the power behind the power of humanity, by default, they should be one of our greatest subjects desired to be studied.

If we can understand our thoughts better, we can unlock many of the outstanding mysteries of our world and our relationship to it. Maybe it is time to review some of Hill's "crazy" theories mentioned in this chapter, and apply modern scientific methods to advance our understanding of our thinking. Ironically, finding better ways to understand our thinking must also start with *a thought*.

Bibliography

Criniti, Anthony M., IV. 2013. The Necessity of Finance: An Overview of the Science of Management of Wealth for an Individual, a Group, or an Organization. Philadelphia: Criniti Publishing.

Criniti, Anthony M., IV. 2014. The Most Important Lessons in Economics and Finance: A Comprehensive Collection of Time-Tested Principles of Wealth Management. Philadelphia: Criniti Publishing.

Criniti, Anthony M., IV. 2016. The Survival of the Richest: An Analysis of the Relationship between the Sciences of Biology, Economics, Finance, and Survivalism. Philadelphia: Criniti Publishing.

Hill, Napoleon. 2011. Think and Grow Rich. United Kingdom: Capstone Publishing Ltd.

ANTHONY M. CRINITI

About Dr. Anthony M. Criniti IV: Dr. Anthony M. Criniti IV (aka "Dr. Finance®") is the world's leading financial scientist and survivalist. A fifth-generation native of Philadelphia, Dr. Criniti is a former finance professor at several universities, a former financial planner, an active investor in diverse marketplaces, an explorer, an international keynote speaker, and has traveled around the world studying various aspects of finance.

He is an award-winning author of three #1 international bestselling finance books: *The Necessity of Finance* (2013), *The Most Important Lessons in Economics and Finance* (2014), and *The Survival of the Richest* (2016). Dr. Criniti is also the host of the highly successful Dr. Finance® Live Podcast as well as one of the top hosts on Clubhouse. Dr. Criniti has started a grassroots movement that is changing the way that we think about economics and finance. Learn more about Doctor Finance at DrFinance.Info.

Author's Website: *www.DrFinance.info*

Book Series Website: *www.The13StepsToRiches.com*

Barry Bevier

KEEP YOUR MIND BRIGHT: YOU'VE GOT TO LOVE YOUR BRAIN

Napoleon Hill likens our brain to a broadcasting and receiving station for thought. Our thoughts are transmitted from one person to another through vibrations in the atmosphere, similar to radio or satellite transmissions. Our brain can be compared to a computer—it has hardware (physiological) and software (neurological). Each must be at its peak for the brain to function at an optimum level. I'm focused on the hardware or physiological aspect of the brain. When we love our brain, we take care of it better, so it serves us better. BRIGHT MINDS is a phrase coined by Dr. Daniel Amen that provides the ingredients to keep the physical aspect of the brain healthy so that the neurological side can function better and age slower.

B **is for Blood Flow**: Blood carries nutrients to every cell in the body and removes toxins. Low blood flow is the number one predictor of Alzheimer's. Research suggests that brain cells don't age; rather, our blood vessels age. Anything that damages circulation restricts getting the nutrients our brains need. So, how do you improve blood flow? Both caffeine and nicotine constrict blood flow to the brain. Limit caffeine: a cup of coffee a day is not a problem. Avoid nicotine. Maintain good blood pressure. As blood pressure goes up, blood flow to your brain goes down.

Take care of your heart. Anything that damages your heart, damages your brain. Exercise at least thirty minutes five times a week, especially walking. Using vibration equipment like PowerPlate for exercise also increases blood flow. Hyperbaric Oxygen Therapy is one of the best ways to increase blood flow and helps improve memory and mood. Many foods increase blood flow like chili peppers, beets, and foods that are high in vitamins E and B. Turmeric, Ginger, and Ginkgo also promote increased blood flow.

R is for Retirement: We often let our brains become less active with age. We can slow and even reverse the aging process to decrease the risks. Things like loneliness, being sedentary, and poor nutrition all accelerate memory loss. Stay connected to people and participate in activities that require new learning. Volunteering is great as it both connects us with others and provides a sense of purpose.

Challenge your brain. When we stop learning, our brain starts dying. Telomeres protect our genes. They are the end caps of chromosomes, like plastic caps on shoelaces. Shortening of telomeres is associated with aging and memory loss, and it is not inevitable. Research shows that lifelong learning, being socially connected (especially volunteering), good nutrition and exercise are all essential to preventing telomere shortening and memory loss. Coordination activities that activate the cerebellum, which is involved with processing speed and memory, are excellent. One of Dr. Amen's favorite activities to keep the brain young is Ping Pong! Pickleball probably fits in there, too!

I is for Inflammation: When you have chronic inflammation, it's like you have a low-level fire destroying your organs, which increases your risk of depression and dementia. High C-Reactive protein and low Omega 3 levels are indicators of inflammation. Having joint pain is a sign of inflammation. The best way to decrease inflammation is to eliminate anything that causes it, such as a diet filled with processed foods and sugar. Maintain good oral health. Research shows gum disease is a major cause of inflammation and memory loss. Cook with turmeric and boost your omega three fatty acids by eating more fish or taking Omega 3 supplements.

G **is for Genetics:** Memory loss runs in families. If you have a family member with Alzheimer's disease or other forms of dementia, that increases your risk. Yet genetic risk is not a death sentence. It is a wake-up call!

One of the major theories about what causes Alzheimer's is a buildup of toxic plaques in the brain. Research has shown that vitamin D, blueberries, sage, turmeric, and green tea can decrease these plaques. If you think you're at risk, early screening is essential. But the most important thing you can do if you have memory problems in your family is to be serious about prevention as soon as possible. Stop making excuses like it's too hard or too expensive to adopt healthier habits—or you will be deprived. Trust me, losing your memory and independence is hard, expensive, and will deprive you and your family of much more.

H **is for Head Trauma:** Our brains are soft, about the consistency of soft butter, and our skulls are hard with multiple sharp bony ridges. Head injuries, even mild ones that may have occurred decades ago, are a major cause of depression, addictions, and memory problems. A study by the Mayo Clinic found that one-third of people who played football at any level had lasting brain damage. If you've had a head injury, the good news is that there are many things you can do to help to heal brain damage. Changing your diet, taking targeted supplements, and doing hyperbaric oxygen therapy can help within a matter of weeks. When you put the brain in a better environment, it will heal.

T **is for Toxins:** One of the most common causes of memory loss and aging is toxins. Besides drugs (including prescription medications) and alcohol, there are many other things that are toxic to your brain, such as smoking and secondhand smoke, mold exposure, carbon monoxide, paint fumes, farm and garden pesticides, heavy metals (including mercury, aluminum, and lead), household cleaning supplies and many personal care products. Lead is found in 60% of lipstick sold in the United States. When the government took lead out of gasoline, it was left in small airplane fuel. A study on one hundred pilots found 70% had toxic-looking brains. Chemotherapy and radiation that is used to kill cancer cells also kills healthy cells.

To decrease your toxin risk, limit your exposure whenever you can. Buy organic to decrease pesticides in foods. Read labels. If a product contains toxic ingredients, don't buy it. What goes on in our body goes into our body and affects our brain. Support the four organs of detoxification: Liver, Kidney, Lungs, and Skin. Drink water, at least half your body weight in ounces per day. Make sure you get plenty of fiber. Sweating from exercise and taking saunas helps detoxify through the skin.

A recent study showed that people who spent lots of time in saunas had the lowest risk of memory problems. Cruciferous vegetables are detoxifying. Support your liver by eating broccoli, cauliflower, cabbage, and Brussels sprouts. Also, here are free apps available to check your personal products and see how toxic they are.

M **is for Mental Health & Movement:** Chronic stress, emotional trauma, depression, bipolar disorder, and ADD have been associated with lasting memory problems. ADD affects nearly 10% of the population and affects both children and adults. Low blood flow in the parts of the brain associated with Alzheimer's is also seen in people with ADD, increasing vulnerability to Alzheimer's. Treating mental health issues does not necessarily mean medicine. Studies have shown that Omega-3 fatty acids, saffron, and other nutraceuticals can help your mood.

Daily movement to get your blood flowing and working up a sweat is essential. Do something you enjoy to increase movement, especially brisk walking. As little as thirty minutes of walking five days a week can have a significant impact. People who can walk three miles an hour have a 90% chance of living to ninety. Those who can only walk one mile an hour have a 90% chance of not reaching ninety. Exercise, meditation, hypnosis, and a vegetable-rich diet help your overall mental health.

I **is for Immunity & Infection:** Recently, a popular celebrity was diagnosed with Alzheimer's, but a second opinion found it was really Lyme disease. Treatment with antibiotics and hyperbaric oxygen healed him quickly. According to the Journal of Alzheimer's Disease, if you struggle with your memory, infectious diseases need to be explored by your physician. Some of the best ways to strengthen your immunity include knowing and optimizing your vitamin D level and taking probiotics, because gut health is critical to your immunity. You should also eat foods such as garlic, onions, and mushrooms.

N **is for Neuro-Hormones:** Hormones are essential for a strong memory. Without healthy hormones, you feel tired and foggy, and your hippocampus (which is involved in cognition and memory functions) will become smaller and weaker. Besides memory, testosterone helps you feel happy, motivated, sexual, and strong. Thyroid gives you energy and mental clarity. Optimizing thyroid improves energy and focus. DHEA helps to fight aging. And, in women, estrogen and progesterone helped boost blood flow. To keep your brain young, keep your hormones healthy. Test every year after the age of forty. Avoid hormone disruptors such as pesticides, phthalates, and parabens in personal products and work with your doctor.

D **is for "Diabesity:"** A double-barreled threat to your memory and involves being diabetic, overweight, or both. Studies show that as your weight goes up, the physical size and function of your brain goes down. With two-thirds of Americans overweight, this is the biggest brain drain in the history of the United States. Excess fat on your body is not innocuous. It disrupts your hormones, stores toxins, and increases inflammation. When obesity is combined with diabetes, the risk is worse. High blood sugar levels damage your blood vessels, which decreases blood flow to the brain.

Food is the key. Here are five simple tips: 1. Eat high-quality calories and not more than you need to maintain a healthy weight. 2. Eat clean protein at every meal to balance your blood sugar and decrease cravings. 3. Focus on healthy fats from fish, nuts, seeds, avocados, and olive and coconut oils that are essential for good brain health. 4. Consume carbohydrates that do not raise your blood sugar, such as those found in colorful fruits and vegetables. Limit sugar and high glycemic carbs such as bread, pasta, potatoes, and rice, which are all inflammatory. 5. Use brain-healthy spices, especially pepper, cinnamon, nutmeg, garlic, cloves, and turmeric. They attack virtually all of the Bright Minds risk factors. When you follow these simple food tips, you can eat incredibly healthy foods that taste amazing.

S is for Sleep & Stem Cells: It is estimated that sixty million Americans have sleep-related issues. Chronic insomnia, sleeping pills, and sleep apnea significantly increase the risk of memory problems. When you sleep, your brain cleans and detoxifies itself. If sleep is poor, toxins build up in your brain and damage your memory. Getting less than seven hours of sleep at night is associated with weight gain, hypertension, accidents, and behavior issues. You can improve your brain tomorrow by improving your sleep tonight.

Alcohol will put you to sleep. However, when it wears off, your brain rebounds and wakes you up a few hours later. To sleep better, make your room cool, dark, and quiet. Avoid electronic devices for one to two hours before bed. Turn off your electronics so they don't disturb you. Listening to music with a specific rhythm can help, as can meditation and EFT (Tapping).

Stem Cells are the building blocks of our bodies and without them, our tissues and organs cannot be renewed, and we would die. Stem Cells can regenerate any type of tissue in the body, including brain cells and neurons. We have the ability to drastically increase the amount of stem cells circulating in our bodies through eating the right foods, taking specialized supplements, fasting, exercise, and hyperbaric oxygen therapy.

To keep BRIGHT MINDS, we only have to follow a few simple, daily practices to have a better brain and the life that goes with it. Make these changes now in your daily routine to enjoy a longer and more healthful life!

BARRY BEVIER

About Barry Bevier: Barry Bevier is a proud father of two amazing daughters, who are pursuing their passions in psychology and architecture in Southern California, where he lived, worked, and raised a family for over forty years. He recently moved to North Carolina to pursue the next adventure in his life's journey. Barry was raised on a family farm near Ann Arbor, Michigan. Growing up, he developed his faith in God, a strong work ethic, a love for nature, and a passion for helping others. After completing his master's degree in civil engineering at the University of Michigan, he pursued a career in engineering, which eventually brought him to Southern California.

In 2000, he married the love of his life, Linda. They shared a beautiful life for ten years, until she succumbed to the effects of lupus and twenty years of treatment with prescription medications. Since then, Barry pivoted his career path into educating and helping others with their health and longevity. Barry has educated himself in alternative, natural modalities in wellness and became a Licensed Brain Health Expert through Amen Clinics. His primary focus and business is a new technology in stem cell supplementation that releases your own stem cells without invasive medical procedures.

Author's Website: *www.BRBevier.stemtech.com*

Book Series Website: *www.The13StepsToRiches.com*

Bonnie Lierse

MY QUIET CHATTER VS. MY QUIET SMALL VOICE: WHO WINS

Thank you, my dear coaches, Erik Swanson, Jon Kovach Jr, and Erin Ley (who introduced me to this mastermind). They awakened my writing abilities and used that part of my brain. I am so deeply and truly blessed that they have inspired that part of my creative abilities.

The brain is an extraordinary vessel that can go way back in time. Tapping into the brain that serves others because of my own self is off the charts. The brain is an extraordinary vessel, one not understood. It is so complex that we do not understand or know how to explain its purpose. Did you know that we are so gifted we do not know half of what we are capable of? I am fortunate, because I have sources and resources, that are contributing to help me. You'll find out soon enough.

We are not as simple in the brain as most think. If you know your gifts, you can become famous and change the world. I am heading toward that DREAM. There are no guarantees in this world, just faith and beliefs. I am a true believer in that. That is my mission in life to serve others in the transition to something major!

I came from a middle-class background and simple upbringing culture in New York City.

I have recently learned about my subconscious mind and very, and I mean very, complex brain. There were questions I had, and I was desperately seeking answers to them.

We need to use many sides of the brain, and when I used to play with a toy, as an example, I never used it for its original purpose. I knew in some way I was creative in some way, shape, or form. When it comes to my grandkids, I need to use a side of creativity that is extremely imaginative, and that is a part of the brain, but I didn't recognize that then.

Yes, this chapter is special because the part of my creative writing is being tapped into and written by a part of myself I did not know even existed. You will figure that out soon by learning about my future life changes—and they are massive!

We know that I was bestowed a special gift for creativity, even back then. You are looking at the one person in the world that now has tremendous insight to view things from a very different perspective. These are things that are not common or that others would understand. My brain is mainly between tapping into my intuition and my gut.

I truly like myself now, for the first time in my life, in my sixties, and am humbled now to write about myself and my brain. I sometimes hear chatter in my brain, and I know that it is telling me something. Did that ever happen to you? There is a part of my brain that has a quiet voice, which is too complicated to explain.

This is all from the chatter side of my brain supporting me, as an author and creator. Truth is, my mind is always chattering, between my ego and my humble self.

What is ego to you? Is it good or not good? For me, I learned a lot from medium readings on my ego. That was and is a wake-up call. When my ego is working overtime, it is so fast-paced that I know there is a list of things I have to do! I am my ego, and it works all the time. At times, I have to tell it to step aside because it then interrupts my purpose and focus! I need my ego to step in and help me. Boy, does my chatter self have energy!

Regarding the brain, Napoleon Hill wrote, "It alone, is the medium through which prayer may be transmitted to the source capable of answering prayer."

Did you know that the conscious, subconscious, and super-conscious minds are a part of you, whether you like it or not? Personally, after what I have learned from studying the mind, I only use a small part of it. Only a small percentage, maybe five percent, use the conscious mind, and many individuals fail because of this.

The subconscious mind uses ninety-five percent of your potential. Many do not know how to access that part of their mind! I am blessed I learned in a unique way, which I will discuss later.

The Primal Brain and the Inner Critic equal the Subconscious. The highest mind is a combination of subconscious and super-conscious.

We are all in charge of our thoughts, and it delves into my creative gifts! You control your fate and you can be in control of your finances. Everything is energy, and that is all there is to it.

> *"Match the frequency of the reality you want*
> *and you cannot help but get it."*
> ~ Albert Einstein

Your thoughts become words; your words become actions; your actions become habits; your habits become your character; your character becomes your destiny.

Now that I have a connection with my chatter self, it is over the top extraordinary because my chatter self is the ego that debates the quiet voice and knows so much more than I do; it balances the weakness that I may have. She, my ego, is strong and powerful and an action-taker, and can be pensive and focused. I can actually hear her in my mind—she converses with me, and it is powerful!

I have changed in personality and built myself esteem, a thousand percent, due to this chatter and ego mind! From day to day, I have a best buddy! We do share stories, like buddies, and it is hilarious because I truly laugh hard at this.

In hindsight, when I look back, I was the quiet, passive, sweet girl. I didn't understand the complexity of the mind then; I really did not understand ego or chatter. I thought confidence was ego, as an example. Now, I understand that it is an inspired peace of mind. I carefully choose the words I select and use, and you know what I mean. I prefer not to use the word try! I thought the word "try" was not the same as attempting, and that trying meant it was never going to happen; however, now, I know it is the start of action.

You are so curious about the small, quiet voice in your mind, and I now am more in-tuned to my quiet, small voice.

I learned about prosperity through my study of the brain. It was eye-opening. We never use most of our brains, and we use only maybe five percent in conscious form. You can access all three but must learn how to access them. Most never tap into the brain beyond the conscious, but I have been blessed to learn this from sources. I found some of my passions, like writing spiritual books for myself and creating children's books that are almost ready to publish.

"You cannot entirely control your subconscious mind, but you can voluntarily hand it over to any plan, desire, or purpose which you wished transformed into concrete form."
~ Napoleon Hill

When I work in leadership or anything, I always look for the creative energy in someone and help them reach their potential. There are many with low self-esteem like I had all my life, but it's taking a new turn and path to change that forever. Many of the young or mature people I work with may not understand they have low self-esteem, but if I can tap into something in them, I am fulfilled.

When I had a dream in my decorating business, I would help bring out the team's best energy, an energy they did not know they had. Wherever I go to Mastermind, I can get a big smile out of someone because they are elated someone has love for them and cares.

I was a member of The Screened Cartoonist Guild. It was one of my favorite graphic design positions. It tapped into my animated side, in a big way. It was such a privilege to do that successfully, and I actually love working with people.

"You have not had time to master faith. Be Patient. Be Persistent."
~ Napoleon Hill

BONNIE LIERSE

About Bonnie Lierse: Bonnie Zaruches Lierse is extremely artistic and creative, with an entrepreneurial bent. Besides that, she is a seasoned agent with more than twenty years of experience in real estate in the New York/Long Island area. She relocated to Northern Virginia in 2012 and continued her real estate career there.

Another passion is creating leaders by working in business leadership development with *Leadership Team Development (LTD)*, and marketing products supplied by *Amway*. She was also a member of *The Screen Cartoonist Guild of Motion Pictures* for many years. Also, she did freelanced for *Sesame Street* in New York City. In addition, she was a District Director for an interior accessory design company, as her own business.

Bonnie is blessed with five beautiful grandchildren and is very close with her children and family, some of whom are also in Virginia. Her missions are leadership, mentorship, paying it forward, and changing lives one at a time. Her motto is *"You* be the difference!"

Author's Website: *www.amway.com/myshop/SplashFXEnterprises*

Book Series Website: *www.The13StepsToRiches.com*

Brian Schulman

IF YOU THINK YOU CAN, YOU CAN

The human brain is a complex and intricate organ that is still not fully understood by scientists and researchers. However, what we do know is that the brain plays a critical role in every aspect of our lives, from our thoughts and emotions to our actions and behavior. It is the hub that makes us human.

As humans, we have the ability to choose our mindset and attitude, which is good news because having a positive mindset and attitude can significantly have a positive impact on our success and fulfillment in life. Thanks to the brain's neuroplasticity, which is the brain's ability to change and adapt over time, we have the ability to train our brains for success and fulfillment!

Research has shown that the brain is capable of forming new neural pathways well into adulthood. That means our brains think and behave in different ways over time, and we can influence these changes. For example, if we want to develop a positive mindset, we can focus on cultivating positive thoughts and behaviors as new pathways are formed in our brain until they become habitual.

One of the ways we can train our brains for positivity is through the practice of gratitude.

Gratitude is a powerful tool that can help us shift our focus away from negative thoughts and emotions towards the things in our lives for which we are thankful, creating positivity. By regularly practicing gratitude, we can rewire our brains to focus on the positive aspects of our lives, rather than dwelling on the negative. The brain cannot simultaneously entertain negative and positive thoughts. By raising our awareness and focusing on the positives in our lives, we spend less time on the negative, and the brain "rewires" itself so that it becomes our new normal (or default mode). The practice can be as simple as naming three things you are grateful for at the end of each day.

Another way to tap into the brain's potential for positive change is through visualization.

Research has shown that visualization can actually activate the same areas of the brain that are activated when we *physically* experience something. This means that by visualizing a desired outcome, we can change our brain to believe that it is possible and increase our motivation to work towards it.

Visualization, also known as manifestation, is the practice of imagining a desired outcome in your mind, as if it has already happened, down to the very last detail. For example, if you want to achieve a certain goal, you can visualize yourself accomplishing that goal, what you are wearing when you do, who is there with you, and experience the feelings that come with successfully achieving what you set out to do.

I can share ideas on "how" to harness the power of the brain, but only you can make it happen!

The importance of self-discipline in achieving success cannot be stressed enough.

Self-discipline is the ability to control our thoughts, emotions, and actions in order to achieve a specific goal by raising our conscious awareness of patterns and actively intercepting no longer helpful thoughts and beliefs. It requires mental strength and focus, which can be developed through practice. It takes time and awareness, setbacks, and resets, but despite failing forward, you must continue to bring your awareness back to your goal and the importance of self-discipline.

One way to develop self-discipline is meditation. The health benefits of meditation are widely documented.

Meditation is a practice that involves training the mind to focus on a specific object or thought, while letting go of distractions and negative thoughts. By practicing meditation regularly, we can strengthen our ability to control and be aware of our thoughts and emotions, which leads to physical changes in the brain, greater self-discipline, and success.

Clients often tell me they can't meditate because they feel as if they're not doing it "right." They attempt to create a practice based upon a movie or magazine article. The reality is that there is more than one way to meditate. Therefore, the chances that you will find success in meditation is higher than you think. Even if you have tried it before, I am going to encourage you to try it again.

My business partner, friend, and amazing coach, Nancy Barrows, patiently guided me to discover my own meditation style and practice. She shared her story with me about being a resistant meditator and how she finally allowed herself to develop her own practice—without judgment. If you ask her about her mediation practice, she will tell you she is a seven-to-fifteen-minute meditator who sits with her legs bent, her back against a chair, music softly playing, incense burning, a rose quartz crystal tucked in her bra against her chest with cats crawling all over her!

Rather than struggling to clear her mind of all thought, she adopted a mantra meditation in which she keeps bringing herself back to the *same* thought while focusing on her breath: "So hum," which is "I am" in Sanskrit. To most people, this doesn't paint the picture we think of as "traditional meditation," but it removed the obstacles that were keeping her from engaging in a consistent meditation practice. And THAT is what matters. Be willing to experiment to find what works for YOU!

In addition to meditation, physical exercise is a health-boosting, effective way to develop self-discipline.

Exercise requires mental focus and the ability to push through physical discomfort, which can translate into other areas of our lives. By consistently pushing ourselves physically, we can develop mental strength and self-discipline and build confidence to help us achieve our goals.

Positive thinking and visualization are important, but they must be accompanied by action in order to produce results and achieve success. Taking action requires courage and confidence, which can be developed through practice and repetition.

Through the practice of "fear-setting," you can gain confidence and take action.

Fear-setting is the process of identifying and analyzing the potential risks and negative outcomes of a particular action or decision, in order to prepare for them and build the confidence to move forward. Once identified, all fears are replaced with positive thoughts for the best outcome.

During the Covid pandemic, I found myself flooded with a tidal wave of emotion. My world was thrust into chaos. Overnight, my mindset became one of fear and negativity, and I struggled to maintain my self-discipline. I was sitting on my couch day after day; my routine of going to work, meeting friends, being out in the world had disappeared. My body was hurting. I needed to move, so I got off the couch and rebuilt my self-discipline by walking.

One step at a time, building up slowly, even when I didn't want to, I took action and made a commitment to myself to walk, especially when I didn't feel like it. Not giving up on myself, I got dressed each day, put on my tennis shoes, and left the house. It wasn't important how much I walked, but that I honored that commitment to myself.

In pushing through my discomfort physically as well as my mental blocks and limiting beliefs, I didn't know I was developing the mental strength I needed to make it through the pandemic, but I felt it. I was physically developing, and had tapped into my brain's neuroplasticity and its ability to change and adapt over time. Through confidence, strength, and courage, I came upon a mantra from within that I would repeat to myself and that would, unbeknownst to me, one day inspire so many others. "If you think you can, you can. If you think you can't, you can. How? One step at a time."

One step and one push-up led to one mile and twenty-five push-ups, which led to 26.4 miles and 800 push-ups. Through practice, repetition, meditation, courage, and confidence, I was able to take action.

By breaking down potential obstacles and developing a plan to overcome them, we can increase our confidence and take action towards our goals.

Arguably, the brain is the most important organ in the human body, responsible for everything from breathing and digestion to emotion and intelligence. It is the central hub of the nervous system, and it's what allows us to perceive, process, and respond to the world around us.

The brain is an incredibly complex organ made up of billions of neurons and glial cells that work together to create the intricate networks that enable us to think and learn. The power of the brain is not limited to just our individual efforts. Our thoughts and beliefs have a powerful impact on the world around us and attract into our lives what we focus on and believe in.

The best part?

Your brain will not only support you—focusing your thoughts and beliefs on abundance, success, gratitude, and action; your brain will *reward* you by making lasting physical changes (neuroplasticity) that lead to enduring positive habits and success!

BRIAN SCHULMAN

About Brian Schulman: Named 'The King Of Community on LinkedIn' by Forbes and known as the Godfather, and Pioneer, of LinkedIn Video and one of the world's premiere live streaming & video marketing experts, Brian Schulman is a 16X #1 Bestselling Author and internationally renowned Keynote Speaker, who's expertise, insights and two Global Award-Winning LinkedIn LIVE Shows have been featured on NASDAQ, Forbes, Thrive Global, Bloomberg, Yahoo Finance, CBS, NBC, FOX, Viacom, Roku TV, Amazon Fire, PODTV, The CW, multiple #1 bestselling books, syndicated on Smart TV Networks & hundreds of shows and podcasts, reaching millions worldwide.

For the last twenty years, Brian has been on a mission to change the landscape of how we do business. Using a heart-centered, growth mindset while leveraging the power of LinkedIn's community and platform, Brian has transformed how business is conducted on LinkedIn worldwide. As the Founder and CEO, through Voice Your Vibe's groundbreaking masterminds and his heart-centered leadership programs, Brian brings his 20+ years of experience, wealth of knowledge and proven leadership expertise to C-Suite Executives and Entrepreneurs globally as an advisor & mentor.

Brian and the Voice Your Vibe Team work with clients strategically to build thought leadership, increase strong brand recognition, grow your network, and create a purpose-driven message that sets you apart from the 1 billion business professionals on LinkedIn.

His focus and dedication to making others feel seen, heard, loved, and valued has earned Brian many honors and awards. Brian has been named a 4X LinkedIn Top Voice, LinkedIn Video Creator Of The Year, 3X Top 50 Most Impactful People of LinkedIn, 4X Rising Star and Influencer To

Watch on LinkedIn, and 2X LinkedIn Global Leader of The Year out of almost 1 billion business professionals on LinkedIn. Brian is also the Executive Producer, Creator, and CoHost of VoiceYourVibe LIVE, which includes two global award-winning weekly LinkedIn LIVE shows broadcast in 120+ countries that have aired for over five years and 500+ consecutive episodes and were named "Best LIVE Festive Show of The Year" at the IBM TV Awards.

Beyond the achievements and accolades, Brian is proudest of his two children and the connections he's made along the way.

Author's Website: *www.VoiceYourVibe.com*

Book Series Website: *www.The13StepsToRiches.com*

Corey Poirier

EXPLORING... THE BRAIN

It's sometimes easy to forget how powerful our brains truly are.

If I'm being honest, I don't challenge my mind nearly enough. My girlfriend does a great job of challenging hers. She plays all kinds of brain challenge games and uses brain development apps.

Me, not so much.

Sure. I write music and books (in which I'm creating the story from scratch). I'm constantly thinking and often creating.

But, when I think about this chapter of *Think and Grow Rich* and what Napoleon Hill suggests, I realize how little I use my brain in such a way that improves my brain's performance.

I mean, he does make the case for using creativity and using social skills, and I'm told by many that it is believed that I have a photographic memory, but I still feel I'm not really challenging my brain enough.

Namely, Hill talks about the importance of brainstorming with others, and I think this is where I'm falling short, as well as where I could work much harder on challenging my brain.

I do have a weekly Mastermind that I run but we haven't been doing brainstorming or hot seats recently.

Working on this chapter reminded me that, although I am likely doing more "brain work" than some, I'm likely falling short on what I could be doing.

That said, that is an easy fix.

I can simply start a brainstorming group or make sure our Mastermind gets back to brainstorming. Perhaps I need to start a specific brainstorming group. Either way, I know the action I should take and it's really not that difficult to take that action.

Where I fall short and don't really know how to make up the difference is in the broadcasting and receiving that Hill describes in *Think and Grow Rich*.

He notes that it is believed that the subconscious mind is the broadcasting (or sending) station, and the creative imagination is the receiving station.

I actually believe it to be true. I believe in energy. I believe that we actually do broadcast to one another. I didn't believe this years ago. I do now.

The challenge is I don't really know how to send or receive signals from or to someone else.

In writing a book about this, one would expect I would say, "Here's how you do this or that," but I want to be transparent and say that this is the chapter in *Think and Grow Rich* with which I struggle to execute.

It is at this point, though, that I ask myself a key question: "Does it matter if I know how to do it as long as I believe it AND understand it?"

For instance, he talked about raising your vibration. Even though I don't know how to do this from a strategy or execution perspective, perhaps I'm already doing it by nature of how positive my energy is and the passion I carry with me each day.

Perhaps in living the way I do, carrying around such positive energy and thinking positive thoughts, I'm already sending out a good vibration that others are picking up on.

Maybe the proof of this is when Hill talks about receiving ideas and thoughts from others.

When I'm sitting down to write a song, more often than not, the words just come to me. I don't have to sit and think about what rhymes with what, or what makes sense. It literally just flows as if it is a gift from someone or somewhere else.

Perhaps this is me receiving those ideas and thoughts from someone else nearby who is transmitting them to me. And if that's the case, maybe I don't need to know how it works; instead, I can just be happy it does and be open to receiving those ideas.

The same thing happens when I'm writing.

I think that I should map it out or outline it beforehand, and yet, whether I'm writing a parable or non-fiction, it just flows.

Maybe I'm already in flow, and because of that, I'm using my brain to send and receive signals.

Perhaps it just is.

I do wish I knew how to do it strategically at times, and I feel like others I speak to feel that can strategically do this—and so perhaps that's why I wonder why I'm not dialed in to the how—but again, maybe I just have to be happy that it is happening for, and to, me.

I do speak to others who look at me like I have two heads, including other songwriters when I tell them the words just come from somewhere.

I thought at times that maybe I'm channeling and maybe it's like the universe or a higher power is sending me the ideas, and if I don't use them, they will go to the next person.

Maybe that is true.

Maybe, though, I'm receiving the words from others nearby who are sending me ideas.

I suppose I'll never know for certain.

Having shared what I have here, perhaps I have also come to a realization myself. What Hill describes in the book is working on some level for me.

Maybe it doesn't matter if I can use my subconscious mind consciously. Maybe I'm already doing it by programming positive thoughts into my mind and by using auto-suggestion.

Maybe I'm already doing enough in the way of using creative imagination.

Maybe I do need to brainstorm more with colleagues.

Maybe I simply need to accept that things are already working the way they are intended to, and all I have to do is keep doing what I'm doing and perhaps add a bit more brainstorming, and I'll be all set.

Maybe I don't need to understand telepathy and the like to benefit from what Hill describes in the book.

Maybe I just used the word maybe many times?

In any case, I hope the take-away from my chapter is that you don't always need to know the answers to get the benefits, and if you do a lot of the right things, the rest will take care of itself.

I know that is what I took of this exploration into my thoughts around *Think and Grow Rich*'s chapter on The Brain.

Now, it's time to give my brain a break.

More directly, it's time for some meditation, my friends.

Until next time, here's to your greater success,

Corey

Facebook: *www.facebook.com/corey.poirier.1/*
LinkedIn: *www.linkedin.com/in/speakercoreypoirier/*
Instagram: *www.instagram.com/thatspeakerguy*
Email: *BluTalksBrand@gmail.com*

COREY POIRIER

About Corey Poirier: Corey Poirier is a multiple-time TEDx Speaker. He is also the host of the top-rated 'Let's Do Influencing' Radio Show, founder of the growing bLU Talks brand, and has been featured in multiple television specials. He is also a Barnes and Noble, Amazon, Apple Books and Kobo Bestselling Author, Award Winning Author, and the co-author of the Wall Street Journal/USA Today Bestseller, *Quitless*.

A columnist with Entrepreneur and Forbes magazine, he has been featured in/on various mediums and is one of the few leaders featured twice on the popular Entrepreneur on Fire show.

He has also interviewed over 6,500 of the world's top leaders, and he has spoken on-site at Harvard and Columbia University, and more recently to Microsoft team leaders and at Inner Circles, which have featured everyone from Brian Tracy to Mark Victor Hansen to Phil Collen (Def Leppard).

Also appearing on the popular Evan Carmichael YouTube Channel, he is a New Media Summit Icon of Influence, was recently listed as the #5 Influencer in Entrepreneurship by Thinkers 360, and listed on the 2021 Brainz CREA Global Awards as an honoree, and he is a Humanitarian Hero Award Nominee, Entrepreneur of the Year Nominee, Champion Award (Business from The Heart) nominee, and to demonstrate his versatility, a Rock Recording of the Year Nominee who has performed stand-up comedy more than 700 times, including an appearance at the famed Second City.

Author's Website: *www.ThatSpeakerGuy.com*

Book Series Website: *www.The13StepsToRiches.com*

Elaine Sugimura

BE WHERE YOUR HEART DESIRES

As I reflect on the earlier chapters that I have written for this book series, *The 13 Steps to Riches,* I am recollecting the moments of failures, successes, power, courage, authenticity, vulnerability, and so much more. The desire to be great at whatever came before me, allowing my subconscious mind to send the messages that led to fulfilling the dreams and goals that have shaped my life thus far, is what has brought me to exactly where I get to be at this point in my life.

As I continue this journey of reinvention/transformation of ME, I am constantly reminded that when I am in my "heart" and not in my "head," magical shifts occur in my life and for others. We are placed on this earth, this one time, so we get to make the most of the experience. Why waste time overthinking any part of your life? What if we chose to dig deep and choose a path of least resistance? What if we challenged ourselves and others to be a stand and source of a transformed world? What if we loved every part of humanity and, one person at a time, caused and created the result we want to see and be in this world? What if we chose to be responsible for everything?

The answers to these questions seem simple, but are they truly? Each of us has experienced what good/bad, right/wrong, blame/shame, fault/guilt feels like. We have all faced these behavioral actions and situations in our lives. For example, I remember the time when I was young and had my share of encounters with each of these specific behaviors. It shaped who I am, and I learned that this is where judgment, assumptions, excuses, and justifications began to grow within me and others. I was asked to "look at" what was driving me towards psychological assessment vs. being in committed action to shift what was not working.

When we judge, when we assume, when we justify, and when we have excuses that we hold onto so dearly—in our personal lives and careers—it is a sign that our vision in life is just not big enough. It means we are allowing our thoughts (brain) to dictate our response. What if we started in our hearts and allowed our choices to be driven from that space?

Each time I reflect about a negative situation and/or reaction I have experienced, I've noticed that the negative thought drove the dissension. What if the choice is to think only positive thoughts and operate from that space? You see, when you allow yourself to see every obstacle as an opportunity, it allows you to confront all the possibilities that exist.

As we learned in earlier chapters of *Think and Grow Rich*, Napoleon Hill speaks to auto-suggestion as an opportunity to shape our subconscious thinking. And when we open ourselves up to all possibilities, our creative imagination begins to take shape and form. Hill continued to state that one must be in vibrational harmony with one's frequency of thought if you are going to attract what one desires.

Our brain transmits and receives all information, and how we process it dictates what gets sent back in return. So, again, the three distinctions that must exist for our brains to transmit properly are: 1. The Subconscious Mind; 2. Creative Imagination; and 3. Auto Suggestion. When we combine these three distinctions with faith, intention, positive emotion, and persistence, possibilities exist! This is when we truly cause and create the results we desire.

Now that I think about all that I have created and experienced in my life, I recognize what worked and what did not work. Identifying what the higher possibilities are allows me to be open and curious, and that leads to further expansion. I am at a crossroads in my life, entering retirement yet reestablishing a business that went dormant during COVID-19. I am asking myself what it is that I want.

Yes, my question to myself is, "What do you want? What do you want? What do you want?" By repeating this key question, it opens and energizes every cell in my body. I feel alive; I feel energized, I feel loved, I feel the power, I feel courageous, and I feel there is more to life than what sits right in front of me. Following my heart, listening to my heart, owning what my heart desires, and creating and manifesting my dreams into reality are what excites me, and there is no end to what I can create. My vision gets to be bigger than life, even at the age of sixty! It is an Attitude, not an Age!

Here is what worked in my life: I focused on what I wanted early in my life. Based on tough circumstances, I chose to remove myself from the drama and begin living the life I wanted to live. I was not seeking a partner but found one by happenstance. Through my desire to create a loving partnership, I found the love of my life. Hiro and I have been married forty years this year and created a family that we are proud to call our own. Life was not always easy, as in sickness and in health, you choose to stand together.

As a two-time breast cancer survivor, I learned a thing or two about survivorship to thriver-ship. I learned to love myself regardless of the scars from my mastectomy. It was a long—very long—road to healing myself of thoughts that did not serve me.

I no longer worry about looking good, being right, perfectionism, or being in judgment of myself or others—as the most important factor is to be aware of who you be! Yes... who you BE! If we are always concerned about others and not aware of how we show up in life, can we really be effective? I know the answer to this for me. The answer is NO, I cannot be effective.

What I have learned is that the bridge between our subconscious mind to our creative imagination is inspiration! When we can inspire ourselves and others around us, life becomes incredibly colorful. What color is your current rainbow? Close your eyes and think of it this way: If your current rainbow is white, black, and grey, what happens to the colors of your rainbow when you are inspired? I can share that for me, my rainbow turns to the colors that reflect my emotions, from pink to every color on the color spectrum.

Inspiration: Blossoming from Surviving to Thriving & Beyond!

This is the title of my latest leadership workshop. I did not recognize it then, but this is the story of my life. The life I chose to create, the life I chose to inspire others, to be in connection with who I am, and what my experiences and wisdom can offer to those who are searching for their very own breakthroughs.

To be a thriver, it takes facing up to the truth, letting go, and surrendering to what does not serve us. It means we get to trust that when we train our brains to think positively, our results will be what we want to attract.

So, why not begin now? LIFE IS NOW. What road do you want to take to find the happiness that awaits? Remember, happiness is an inside game. It is up to you to cause and create the result you want to attract. Be responsible for all of it, everything you manifest in your life. Know that when you are authentic, vulnerable, radically honest, courageous, confident, powerful, loving, passionate, and compassionate, there is no better place, as these ways of being are what make the world go around.

I want to leave you with a few powerful quotes that I live by. Remember that if you allow your showman to live on the 15th floor (your head) vs. heading down to the first floor (your heart), you are missing out on life. Everything happens the moment the door opens on the first floor. Take the risk, lean in, confront whatever it is you have been avoiding, experience whatever it is that you get to experience, and then choose. Choose powerfully, and you will manifest your dream into reality.

"The desire to reach the stars is ambitious. The desire to reach hearts is wise."
~ Maya Angelou

"Imagination is everything. It is the preview of life's coming attractions."
~ Albert Einstein

"Whatever we plant in our subconscious mind and nourish with repetition and emotion will one day become reality."
~ Earl Nightingale

Here is my last manifestation quote I would love to share:

*"What you think, YOU BECOME
What you feel, YOU ATTRACT
What you imagine, YOU CREATE."*
~ Buddha

Lastly, I want to thank the key trainers who have shaped who I am today: Michael Strasner, Lisa Kalmin, Lynne Sheridan, Myrna Gonzalez, Judith Rich, AJ Leto, Chris Hawker, Mary Jo Foster, and many mentors, coaches, and friends. Thank you from the bottom of my heart.

ELAINE SUGIMURA

About Elaine R. Sugimura: Elaine is an accomplished CEO turned Business Consultant / Life Strategist who has a passion for creating Leaders amongst Leaders. With over thirty-five-plus years in the fashion and food and beverage industry, she has a passion for not only leading but also supporting those who are seeking to reinvent who they are no matter where they are in life. She is a two-time breast cancer survivor and she knows a thing or two about surviving to thriving.

Fun fact: she is an adrenaline junkie—the higher, the faster, the better. Her love for adventure has led her to travel to many parts of the world by plane, train, and automobile. She and her husband, Hiro, share their home in Northern California. They have raised two extraordinary sons, Bryce and Cole, and have added two beautiful daughters-in-law, Erica and Giselle, to their growing family. Her legacy is to share what is possible when we open ourselves up to the issues that hold us back. Her life's mission is to move those who are just surviving into Thrivers!

Author's Website: *www.ElaineRSugimura.com*

Book Series Website: *www.The13StepstoRiches.com*

Elizabeth Anne Walker

WIRED FOR SAFETY: ADAPTING TO SUCCESS

Growth should be your number one value! Stop procrastinating! Believe in yourself! Self-love is the key! You need a growth mindset over a fixed mindset! Become the best version of yourself! *Think and Grow Rich!* Million-dollar funnels! 100 million dollar offers! Awaken now!

These are all catch cries of an ever-growing personal development industry set to be a $4.2 Billion industry in the next few years. Let's face it: it is an industry with all the right values and ideals; however, there are two very valuable pieces of information that are omitted from nearly every personal development course or seminar out there.

OUR BRAIN ISN'T WIRED FOR SUCCESS! IT IS WIRED FOR SAFETY!

It is an incredibly primitive organ that is specifically useful to keep us safe, to provide the fight or flight reactions, to have a memory, and to keep us safe.

Well, I ask you, how is doing something new and different even remotely safe? You see, our brain knows this because we've programmed it in a particular way, day in and day out, to keep us safe. So, when we decide to do something new, we must convince ourselves that it's okay. Initially, we do that in our conscious mind. We tell ourselves that we are brave, that we are smart, and that if others can do it, so can we. We read books, consume content, and ask our friends, and if we're one of the lucky ones, we actually start.

The thing is, luck is a by-product of being okay with less safety. Risk-taking behavior is discouraged by our brain, both consciously and unconsciously. This is how some people have a great idea and never get that idea off the ground. It's not because they aren't brave, it's not because they aren't smart, it's because the programs in their brain are wired for safety rather than success.

The amygdala is the beautiful part of our brain, the ancient part of our brain that is wired to look for danger. In the times of cavemen, looking for danger was important. It was the difference between life and death. However, desperate to hold on to its former useful glory, if we experience one hurdle, and it upsets us or scares us, our brain labels it as negative and stores a memory around it. This is what creates the fight or flight response the next time you encounter that again!

This organ that we grow up feeding information is often fed information that enhances our fear rather than information that feeds our success. Imagine wanting to be successful and then learning about wars, the fall of nations, famine and starvation, economic collapse, and environmental disasters.

Essentially, our whole schooling life is made up of learning things that were negative in the past and postulating how these things may have been better or can be better in our future. We are set up! Our brain is essentially hijacked from the time we are five years old until we are eighteen—sometimes even longer! To be upstanding citizens and learn all the reasons why we need to be careful and thoughtful!

I remember a time when I was sixteen years old, and my class was looking at the environmental impact of a highway running through an Australian Bush corridor. The rhetoric of the teacher was very pro-environment and anti-highway. Consequently, most of the girls in my class wrote an essay supporting the environment.

I had been taught from a young age to think differently, to be defiant, and to question what I was taught. I wrote my essay on the future benefits of the highway, and, of course, I included a planting of trees program; however, rather than relying on environmental impact studies of the day, I looked outside the square towards population growth trends, which showed that it was obvious that a highway built at the time would serve a burgeoning population within three years, cutting hours off their city journey and thus having a positive impact on the environment.

The essay I wrote was given a fail by my teacher. I was an A-grade student. So, I took my essay to the principal and asked her to explain where I had gone wrong other than disagreeing with my teacher. The principal asked for two weeks—I imagine she went away and did some research herself. I was never called back in; however, on my report card, I received an A+. Some labeled that bravery on my part. I labeled it as risk-taking, and consequently, my brain created a program and belief that allowed it to take risks and, therefore, create success.

Some of my family called me defiant. My grandfather said I had a great use of the art of intuition. Interestingly, our brain is so obsessed with safety that it looks for things that are outside our normal awareness and sometimes labels them dangerous, yet when we question the danger or act prior to the danger being realized. We call it—that second sense of knowing that we know.

Once we combine the principles of intuition and positive risk-taking and add to them future pacing, we start the process of our brain being able to recognize that success is possible. Future pacing is setting goals that are future-focused, utilizing the resources not only of today but also those postulated for the future.

Using our intuition is a combination of brain, heart, and gut, where we listen to the messages our physical and spiritual bodies are sending us. Risk-taking, fraught with danger, is the very thing that allows us to build resilience in the present. As soon as we know that our risk was worth it, our brain starts looking for the next calculated risk. The more pro-risk we are the more successful we are. The more risk-averse we are the less successful we are.

So, how do we rewire our brain for success? Firstly, we must learn to trust our gut and the messages from our body. Secondly, we must learn to trust the musings of the spirit, the place where all ideas come from. Thirdly, we must be prepared to take a risk when our entire body and brain, as well as those surrounding us, are encouraging us to be safe.

As we continue to take risks, trust our intuition, and believe in energetics that are outside of us, yet connected to us, our brain does some interesting things. First of all, we get a dopamine release, and this makes us feel good. If the risk is large enough, we get an adrenaline release, which provides a quick rush and intense feelings of pleasure.

What's most interesting is that in studies done in the UK, the lower the grey matter in the brain, the higher the propensity for risk-taking behaviors, which completely eliminates the limiting belief that "I'm not smart enough." Even more interesting is another study that found that associated with risky behavior were 124 genetic variants located on 99 separate regions of the genome.

If I were to think logically about this, a brain that has so many centers via genetics for risk-taking behavior must be a brain that recognizes the value of risk-taking behavior. And as we retrain our brain, we can retrain our results.

The most exciting part of all of this is that our brain is malleable. That means we can teach ourselves to be successful by training our brains. You've probably heard about fixed mindset and growth mindset. I'd like to postulate something new, creative, imaginative mind flow. You see, whenever the mind is set, nothing changes.

In creative imaginative mind flow, failure becomes as important as success, and risk with reward becomes the goal. Creative imaginative mind flow is the way of the future where failures are celebrated, and growth is a given. Where success is commonplace because failure is merely a stop on the way.

Love—For Self & Others

Love is one of the most powerful emotions that humans can experience. It has the ability to bring people together and create a sense of connection that is unparalleled. However, love is not just about romantic relationships. It is also about the love we have for ourselves and the love we have for others.

Loving ourselves can be one of the hardest things to do, but it is crucial for our well-being. When we love ourselves, we are more confident, resilient, and able to navigate life's challenges with greater ease. It is important to practice self-love regularly by taking care of ourselves physically, mentally, and emotionally.

Loving others means treating them with kindness, compassion, and respect. It means acknowledging their strengths and weaknesses and accepting them for who they are. It is about building strong relationships with family, friends, and community members. By loving others, we create a positive impact on the world around us.

Love is a powerful force that has the ability to transform our lives and is imperative to our self-development. By practicing self-love and loving others, we can create a more fulfilling and meaningful existence.

ELIZABETH ANNE WALKER

About Elizabeth Walker: Elizabeth is Australia's leading Female Integrated NLP Trainer, an international speaker with Real Success, and the host of Success Resources (Australia's largest and most successful events promoter, including speakers such as Tony Robbins and Sir Richard Branson) inaugural Australian Women's Program "The Seed." Elizabeth has guided many people to achieve complete personal breakthroughs and phenomenal personal and business growth. With over twenty-five years of experience transforming the lives of hundreds of thousands of people, Elizabeth's goal is to assist leaders to create the reality they choose to live, impacting millions on a global scale.

A thought leader who has worked alongside people like Gary Vaynerchuck, Kerwin Rae, Jeffery Slayter, and Kate Gray, Elizabeth has an outstanding method of delivering heart with business.

As a former lecturer in medicine at the University of Sydney and lecturer in nursing at Western Sydney University, Elizabeth was instrumental in the research and development of the stillbirth and neonatal death pathways, ensuring each family in Australia went home knowing what happened to their child, and felt understood, heard, and seen.

A former Australian Champion in Trampolining and Australian Dance sport, Elizabeth has always been passionate about the mindset and skills required to create the results you are seeking.

Author's Website: *www.ElizabethAnneWalker.com*

Book Series Website: *www.The13StepsToRiches.com*

Erin Ley

LIGHT UP YOUR LIFE

In *Think and Grow Rich*, Napoleon Hill said, "The author working in conjunction with the late Dr. Alexander Graham Bell and Dr. Elmer R. Gates, observed that every human brain is both a broadcasting and receiving station for the vibration of thought. In a fashion like that employed by the radio broadcasting principle, every human brain can pick up vibrations of thought which are being released by other brains."

The brain is a complex organ in the human body which orchestrates intelligence, interprets the senses of sight, smell, touch, sound, and taste, initiates movement of the body, and controls our behavior.

The brain is like a computer. It receives information from the senses and body, processes it, and sends messages back to the body. The human brain, though, is so much more powerful than a computer. We can think and experience emotions, which is the foundation of human intelligence.

Bob Proctor talks about these six creative mental faculties:

1. Perception
2. Reason
3. Will
4. Memory
5. Imagination
6. Intuition

We can tangibly see the brain. The mind is not physical, so no one has ever actually seen it. The higher creative mental faculties are intangible and cannot be measured nor described fully.

In the book, *Think and Grow Rich*, Napoleon Hill states, "The operation of your mental broadcasting station is a comparatively simple procedure. You have but three principles:

1. Subconscious Mind: The Sender
2. Creative Imagination: The Receiver
3. Auto-Suggestion: The medium between the two

"Creative Imagination is the receiving set of the brain which receives thoughts released by the brains of others. It is the agency of communication between one's conscious, or reasoning mind, and the fore sources from what one may receive thought stimuli. When stimulated or stepped up to a high rate of vibration, the mind becomes more receptive to thought, which reaches it through outside sources. This stepping-up process takes place through positive emotions or negative emotions. Through the emotions, the vibrations of thought may be increased.

The Subconscious mind is the sending station of the brain through which vibrations of thought are broadcast. Creative Imagination is the receiving set through which the energies of thought are picked up.

Auto Suggestion is the medium by which you may put into operation your broadcasting station. Through Auto Suggestion, this is where Desire may be transmuted into its monetary equivalent."

In 1991, I began my journey in the personal development realm. After working on Wall Street, fully licensed for a few years, not knowing anything about the "inner world," I was diagnosed with non-Hodgkins lymphoblastic lymphoma, a rare pediatric cancer, at age twenty-five.

The doctors informed me that if the chemotherapy didn't work as fast as the tumor was growing, I'd be dead in a month. As the two-and-a-half-year protocol began in June of 1991, I was introduced to self-development books. Up until that point, I looked to the outer world for validation for everything. I thought my insides were just what I learned about in fifth-grade science, encompassing the organs, including the brain, skeletal system, and so on. Even my faith in God was outside of me, up in the sky somewhere.

Then my whole world changed, my life was rocked, and my mind was blown open. The love I began to feel for myself and others cannot be put into words. The gratitude and appreciation I felt for every little thing began to take over my mind. The fear I felt in the beginning began to dissipate. The Grim Reaper took a back seat, and my heart and mind began to be filled with those goals not yet accomplished.

I read a transformative book early in the diagnosis called *Full Catastrophe Living* by Jon Kabat-Zinn, which introduced me to mindfulness meditation, and I loved it. This book dealt with every stressor in life imaginable.

Speaking of imagination, the other powerful, life-transforming book I read at that time was *Creative Visualization* by Shakti Gawain. This book illustrated the significance of having a crystal-clear vision for your life and to visualize it as if it was happening right then and there.

When I married meditation with visualization, my whole life changed. I got into the driver's seat of my own life, as opposed to life driving me; I no longer allowed the outer world to dictate who I was and how successful I'd become. It was an extraordinary awakening, and my health began to improve drastically at a rapid pace. The doctors were, and still are, scratching their foreheads wondering how I was able to escape death on multiple occasions during the grueling protocol.

When I wrote the book, *THE WILL TO LIVE: The Perks of Cancer Through the Eyes of a Survivor*, I discussed and illustrated how powerful our brain, including the mind, really is. As a Life Coach and Business Strategist for the last thirty years, I've taught my clients how to rewire the brain and reprogram the subconscious. Back in the nineties, very few people were talking about this, and the doctors nicknamed me *The Miracle Maker*. They began having their patients call me at home in the

1990s, and that's how I started coaching. The doctors did not understand, nor could they convey to their patients what I was doing.

The subconscious mind is what runs our life. Whatever we take on as beliefs is what we live out. So, what we repeatedly think about is what gets deposited in the subconscious. We literally become what we think about.

Creative imagination is when ideas come to us. Some say the ideas come from the ether; I say they come as a Divine Download. These ideas do not have to be logical. As a matter of fact, when designing the goals you'd like to achieve, and writing out a crystal-clear vision for your life, you want them to be beyond your wildest imagination. The sky is just the beginning. Whether you dream big or small, you will get what you expect. So, please toss logic to the wind when writing out what you want and allow your creative imagination to provide you with the inspired ideas to get you there.

Auto-Suggestion is necessary to override the programming you have that no longer serves you. You may have taken on beliefs as a child that are keeping you limited and stuck in self-doubt. Auto-suggestion is when you repeatedly think about something, hear something, or speak about something, which then makes an imprint in the brain of what is super important to you and needs to be lived out. Many people acquire self-limiting beliefs without even knowing it and do not understand why their life is so difficult.

Reprogramming the subconscious is simple, not easy. You must be intentional about guarding your thoughts carefully and only speaking into what you want in life, repeatedly. Through repetition of the empowered thoughts and words, you will begin to override the victim mentality you were carrying around all this time without knowing it.

Gratitude and appreciation are the bridge from fear to love, and you will begin to live an abundant life of love, relationships, money, health, and spirituality—anything you decide you want. What we focus on expands, so focus on what will bring you to your desired destiny. Only you can make that happen. Tune in to the empowered loving thoughts and watch the people, places, and experiences come to you, helping you get to where you want to be. This is the beauty of the human brain and the potential of every single person on this planet, regardless of circumstances. Circumstances can be changed in an instant. When you change your thoughts, your life changes, instantly.

I'm living my best life these days, and I have a morning routine that helps prime my brain. These are the four powerful things I say and do before leaving my home and venturing out into the world:

1. When I wake up, I say, "Thank you, God (for everyone and everything)! I have sixteen hours of pure potential and endless opportunities in front of me before going back to sleep. I can't wait to see the people, places, and experiences You have in store for me today."

2. As a Life Coach and Business Strategist, I look forward to seeing whose life I can transform for the better today.

3. I shower off my energy from yesterday for a fresh start.

4. As I get dressed, I play my musical playlist and dance around my room to get my body and mind going at the same time.

I would love to hear what your morning routine is. If you don't have one, I'd love for you to contact me at www.ErinLey.com to discuss how you can start living your best life. Since 1991, my mantra has always been, "Celebrate life, and you'll have a life worth celebrating!" Have a magnificent day, and always remember to live onward and upward!

ERIN LEY

About Erin Ley: As Founder and CEO of Onward Productions, Inc., Erin Ley has spent the last thirty years as an Author, Professional Speaker, Personal and Professional Empowerment, and Success Coach predominantly around mindset, vision, and decision. Founder of many influential summits, including "Life On Track," Erin is also the host of the upcoming online streaming T.V. show, "Life On Track with Erin Ley," which is all about helping you get into the driver's seat of your own life.

They call Erin "The Miracle Maker!" As a cancer survivor at age twenty-five, single mom of three at age forty-seven, and successful Entrepreneur at age fifty, Erin has shown thousands upon thousands across the globe how to become victorious by being focused, fearless, and excited about life and your future! Erin says, "Celebrate life and you'll have a life worth celebrating!"

To see more about Erin and the release of her fourth book, "WorkLuv: A Love Story," along with her "Life On Track" Course and Coaching Programs, please visit her website.

Author's Website: *www.ErinLey.com*

Book Series Website: *www.The13StepsToRiches.com*

Fatima Hurd

HIGHER FREQUENCY

The Brain is a magnificent and incredible organ where the true magic begins. The brain is where thoughts filter through into the creative faculty and begin the creative process that Napoleon Hill refers to in *Think and Grow Rich*.

Although our brain is responsible for many functions, I want to focus on thoughts, decisions, and emotions. These functions are relevant to the conscious up-leveling of our life. When we are vibrating at a low frequency, we are closing ourselves off from receiving ideas from the ether that can help us fulfill our purpose.

When we are in higher frequency or energy, our emotions are aligned with the ideas that are coming through. In the book about Faith of this series, I mentioned how I manifested my husband and how I was intentional with having a man in my life that bonded and loved my son (from a previous relationship) like his own. The idea came to me, and the mental image that came through is what I wrote on a piece of paper.

As I wrote it, my emotions were aligned with the idea of what kind of father I thought or felt my son deserved. I wrote the words down as my thoughts, which flowed easily and effortlessly on the paper. The idea came when I changed my state of being from low to high vibration.

Even though, at the moment, being in a relationship with someone was not the initial thought, the DESIRE to have a father figure in my son's life, someone he could love, trust, and bond with, was more important to me than anything in the world. My experience as a child not having my real father in my life and not having a father figure that supported me and protected me created many problems for me in the future associated with not being enough, and that is not what I wanted for my son.

Again, everything begins in the brain. At that moment, when I had created a mental image of the father figure I wanted for my son through autosuggestion, the hypothalamus was producing oxytocin. This love hormone acted like a volume dial, turning up and amplifying brain activity related to whatever I was experiencing at that moment—which was hope, the certainty that my son deserved nothing less than an extraordinary father figure in his life. This also meant that I deserved to find love, too.

As you know, the universe delivered, and I took immediate action, as Divine intervention would have it. A friend told me about E-Harmony and suggested I should sign up. My world was my son, Brandon, so I didn't go out and had every excuse not to go out. I was doing an internship at CBS Radio for 94.1, doing voiceovers and broadcasting live from different venues, which was fun, but kept me busy. The rest of the time, I just wanted to be with my son, and this schedule was eliminating all opportunities for me to find someone.

I wasn't sure how I felt, but I decided to move forward and sign up for E-Harmony. I think it took two days to fill out the *About You* section. I realized it was all physiological. I had to keep answering questions that were written differently to see if you answered them the same as potential matches. I guess this is how they aligned you with the right person, which works because when I was done, I got what they call a "nudge" from my now husband, saying he liked my profile. And if you read *Faith* in this series, you'll know what happened. We have been together for thirteen years and married eleven this year.

Even though life was not ideal when I created my vision board, my gratitude, and love for my son, my family, especially my mom—who didn't hesitate once when I had to move in with her—and my siblings, who all showed up for my son and kept me at a higher vibrational frequency. In my heart, I knew that whatever I was going through was temporary; that if it were meant to be, it would be up to me. Being in that frequency allowed my brain to produce the thought of love and helped me create a mental picture of how that looked for Brandon and me. All the pieces came together, and that was one of my most successful years of manifesting. I went on to find a job that paid twice as much as the job I was laid off from.

The brain is where that magic begins. The brain is not a muscle but an organ, and we need to train it like a muscle. Fitness for your brain is important—your mind only gets stronger if you work on it. I've been on this journey of self-development and spiritual work for years.

It took grit, commitment, and the knowing that my failures were nothing more than lessons that have put me on the path to success. This meant taking accountability for everything that happened to me or my life and making a conscious decision to keep going and trust the process, even if it meant not knowing at the time what the outcome would be.

"Whatever the mind of man can conceive and believe it can achieve."
~ Napoleon Hill

Your brain is powerful, so what you feed can serve you or destroy your mindset is everything.

We are the authors of our lives, and we get to choose what we want that to look like. As I up-leveled my mindset, my thoughts have leveled as well. This journey began many years ago when my life was turned upside down and turned out to be a blessing in disguise; it started with a self-development book, and now I surround myself with only winners and shakers and people who are where I want to be next level.

FATIMA HURD

About Fatima Hurd: Fatima is a personal brand photographer and was featured in the special edition of *Beauty & Lifestyle's* mommy magazine.

Fatima specializes in personal branding photographs dedicated to helping influencers and entrepreneurs expand their reach online with strategic, creative, inspiring, and visual content. Owner of a digital consulting agency, Social Branding Digital Solutions, Fatima helps professionals with all their digital needs.

Fatima holds ten years of photography experience. An expert in her field, she hosts workshops to teach anyone who wants to learn how to use and improve their skills with DSLR and on manual mode.

Hurd is also a mother of three, wife, certified Reiki master, and certified crystal healer. She loves being out in nature, enjoys taking road trips with her family, and loves meditation and yoga on the beach.

Author's Website: *www.FatimaHurd.com*

Book Series Website: *www.The13StepsToRiches.com*

Frankie Fegurgur

GET FIT TO GET RICH AT ANY AGE

Most people are doing it backward. They neglect their health their entire career, running off caffeine and sugar, hoping to retire at 65 with enough to scrape by. Many make futile attempts to buy back their youth with the latest trend. Many more battle cardiovascular disease, cancer, and dementia. Prescription drugs prolong their lifespan, but those who survive will likely be left penniless. People sacrifice their health now in hopes that a higher income will make up for it. A greater net worth will indeed unlock access to fancy gym memberships and even personal chefs.

Sadly, the data suggests that decades of chronic stress and a sedentary lifestyle are insurmountable for most people. Your greatest chance to build an active body is now. You will never be this young again, and odds are you'll never be this healthy either. It is a fallacy to believe that we will be in total control of our minds and bodies up until the very end.

I've witnessed cognitive decline in some of my clients, and it's heartbreaking. It starts seemingly harmless, such as misplacing a financial document or not showing up to an appointment. Sometimes, soon after, they begin to forget the names of family members and repeat themselves constantly. I've even had a client get off the phone with me, just to call right back, and ask me the same question as if we had never spoken.

While the focus of this chapter is empowering those aged 55+ to keep their brains healthy, this information is beneficial for everyone. Parents

133

must ensure that their children are well-adapted to stress, or else they will be unable to cope with distraction, anxiety, and depression. I do not subscribe to the helicopter parent mentality—it creates the opposite of self-regulating young people. Facing obstacles is normal. Adopting healthy habits in early adversity means that negative outcomes can be mitigated and even a catalyst for growth. These habits are priceless as the world becomes more complicated.

I've spoken at length about the ever-expanding sandwich generation. This group balances the demands of caring for aging parents while also raising children. The phenomenon has ballooned over the last few years; the same group is supporting their grandparents on one side, and their now adult children and even grandchildren on the other. Problems in either generation or with your wellness and finances will impact the others.

Where I see this most often is senior financial abuse. Over $3 billion was stolen from seniors last year. These scams are increasingly complex, and recovering stolen funds is nearly impossible. Be sure to talk to them about trending crimes, such as phishing scams through text and email. If they seem to lack comprehension or have been scammed multiple times, it could be an early warning sign of their brain health.

If there is evidence of elder financial abuse, contact their local county senior services office and the attorney general's office. Before any of that can happen, please put protection in place. Having the right financial and estate planning will secure their legacy and prevent a lot of sleepless nights. Ideally, your best plan is to keep your loved ones as mentally sharp as possible.

Researchers are just beginning to understand how there are seniors in their 80s whose brainpower competes with those decades younger. Even when it takes them longer to learn something, they can still master it. This goes against the previously limiting belief that you will only decline with age.

Most seniors will be unwillingly phased out of their jobs. They'll struggle with a loss of identity and purpose. Back when they punched a clock, their schedule was largely dictated by their employer. Instead of seeing this next stage as a new beginning, they see it as an act of decline. Instead of pursuing ideas and passions that they previously never had time for, they become homebodies. They quit trying. They think they know it all. A sedentary mentality creeps in, and as their health declines, they become isolated. Life doesn't have to end this way.

Imagine being sixty-five years old and earning more in the next ten years than you did in the previous forty-plus years of working. What if you could build income streams that allowed you to work if you wanted to, and not because you had to? I'm talking about finding a renewed purpose that lights up your brain in ways you may never have experienced when at a job just "pulling down a check."

The foundation for this success is not what you've been told. The key is exercise. Your physical fitness is directly related to your financial fitness. Next time you're in a money-making slump, evaluate what your exercise has been like in the weeks prior. Go for a good run and see if your brain doesn't fire off with new ideas. There are plenty of ways to incorporate fitness into your routine, even if you've never done it before.

One of my favorite ways is through resistance training. Lifting weights can strengthen your bones and increase your range of motion, which in turn prevents debilitating falls. If an elderly person can't lift weights, then cardio will still provide brain-protecting benefits. Beyond the benefits of stronger bones, more muscle, and a toned physique, exercise has tremendous cardiovascular benefits.

Most people have realized that poor cardiovascular health leads to diabetes, heart disease, and stroke. What many people still don't realize is that it also leads to cognitive decline and even dementia. Being physically and mentally fit will save you hundreds of thousands of dollars in long-term care costs. Long-term care is often as simple as needing assistance with the activities of daily living, such as bathing and eating.

But for more serious ailments, the cost easily exceeds $10,000 a month. Even retirees with an excellent net worth will run out of money due to medical issues, especially when occurring at the beginning of their retirement. Changes in the brain can now be detected a decade before the damage occurs. If a person isn't proactively managing their health, they won't know until it's too late.

This is markedly true for people without the financial means to afford cutting-edge testing and treatment. Many people falsely believe that they can rely on Medicare to cover their health expenses. Unfortunately, federal health insurance has restrictions on which medications and care you're eligible for. They do not cover memory care, nursing homes, or anything around the clock. In-home care by family is not necessarily cheaper and brings an entirely new set of challenges, such as constricted quality of care, declining health of the caregiver, and sacrifice of wages.

Exercise alone may not be enough to prevent dementia, particularly in the presence of significant underlying genetic factors. But no one wants to reach the end of their life knowing they could have done more. Exercise is hope for the brain. It creates a healthy loop by taking action and building momentum.

It doesn't have to be boring or lonely. Exercising with friends and family outdoors is a priceless way to ensure accountability and build relationships. There's no wonder why marathons and obstacle courses are so popular. Overcoming challenges like climbing up walls and swinging across pits of mud gives you the confidence to tackle all types of challenges in your business and your relationships.

I understand that this approach is not for everyone. Some seniors prefer to slow down or need low-impact activities. One simple and affordable way to stay sharp is by playing with puzzles. Solving puzzles reduces stress, increases focus, improves reasoning skills, and even prevents memory loss.

Even if healthier choices did nothing but delay the onset of symptoms, it would be priceless. One of the lesser-known causes of dementia is excessive sugar consumption. Sugar wreaks havoc on our blood vessels, causing them to shrink and carry less oxygen to our brains.

Approximately forty percent of Americans are prediabetic and don't know it. Cutting your sugar intake could save your life.

I'm only somewhat joking when I say that I want to stay healthy long enough until the robot body parts can take over. I've always believed that everything from computers that interface with our brains, nanobots that monitor and heal our genes, and even full-on exoskeletons will soon enhance our capabilities and longevity. This may sound a little too sci-fi for you, but we already see examples in the form of pacemakers and hearing aids. Other implementations on the fringe include an implanted wireless tag to prove your identity and a remote-activated insulin pump.

Some ideas may be downright silly, but others will revolutionize medicine. I don't mean just living longer, I mean a substantially higher quality of life. Many of my clients have seen improvements in their health because of a reduction in stress, more meaningful connections, newfound freedom, and passion for the future. It starts with compassionately asking yourself: What can I do today to be physically and mentally strong enough for what lies ahead?

FRANKIE FEGURGUR

About Frankie Fegurgur: Frankie's "burning desire" is helping people retire with dignity. Frankie distills the lessons he has learned over the last fifteen years and empowers our youth to make better financial decisions than the generation before them. This is a deeply personal mission for him—he was born to high-school-aged parents, and money was always a struggle. Frankie learned that hard work alone wasn't the key to financial freedom and sought a more fulfilling path. Now, he serves as the COO of a nonprofit financial association based in the San Francisco Bay Area, teaching money mindfulness. He, his wife, and their two children can be found exploring, volunteering, and building throughout their community.

Author's Website: *www.FrankMoneyTalk.com*

Book Series Website: *www.The13StepsToRiches.com*

Fred Moskowitz

IT ALL STARTS WITH GETTING INTO THE FEELING OF FEELING GOOD

The way that we feel impacts virtually everything that we do. It impacts how we take on a new project, the work we perform in our business or our profession, and creative work. Most importantly, it impacts the way we show up in our relationships. We integrate the energy that is inside us, no matter good or bad, into every activity, encounter, and situation in our lives. The **thoughts** that we focus on create the **feelings** that we have, which gets applied to the **effort** that we put forth (which is energy), which then goes into the **actions** that we take, and finally, that gets us the **results** that we experience.

THOUGHTS > FEELINGS > EFFORT > ACTIONS > RESULTS

Keeping these concepts in mind, it becomes easy to understand how—if we want to achieve better results—we can start out by getting into the feeling of feeling good, which kicks off the chain reaction. In this chapter, I will share some actionable ways that can help you to be aware of how you feel and make some changes, if necessary, before you begin any project, task, or activity.

Experiencing Gratitude as a Habit

I like to begin by getting into gratitude on a daily basis. The feeling of gratitude can be one of the most powerful emotions, and an added benefit is that it displaces negative thoughts. Take steps to make gratitude a regular practice, whether you feel good or not, especially when you are feeling upset or "less than glorious," or when you are feeling bad with negative thoughts spiraling out of control. When things start to go into a loop of negativity, you can benefit from a pattern interrupt.

Have you ever heard the notion that what you focus on will expand? With this in mind, start to think about the things for which you have gratitude. Start small, and make a list using paper and pen. I will share with you some examples: my health, the nutritious meal that I enjoyed for lunch, the great phone call I had today with a colleague where we connected at a deeper level, the opportunity to say hello to my mom, the business deal that just completed, the powerful computer I get to work on while I write this chapter, the safe place where I live, my wonderful family that is always there for me, and the powerful mentors that have positively influenced me over the past months.

After you go through this exercise and make your own list, review each item, and hold the feeling of gratitude in your heart for a moment. I guarantee that you will start to feel better each time that you do this. In fact, consider about what kind of impact it would have if you did this exercise every day. I stress the importance of using a pen and paper to write down your list. The act of putting a physical pen to paper will simultaneously engage the brain, hands, and heart, and it will establish that mind and body connection, while at the same time strengthening the neural pathways.

Meet Oxytocin, the Love Hormone

Perhaps you have heard about a hormone naturally produced in our bodies called oxytocin. Oxytocin is released into the body through things like physical touch, music, and exercise. This hormone is produced by the pituitary gland and released into the bloodstream. It is a powerful chemical which can help us to bond with loved ones and makes us feel good. Think about the special bond and deep connection that forms between a mother and her newborn child: this happens largely as a result of oxytocin.

Oxytocin is also produced when we feel physical attraction to a romantic partner, when we fall in love. This is why it is sometimes known as "the love hormone."

Another way to increase oxytocin in the body is through exercise. Many studies have been able to measure increased oxytocin levels in participants immediately following high-intensity exercise training.

Music, especially experiencing live music, is another way to boost our oxytocin levels. Whether playing and performing music in a group setting or experiencing a live music performance in person, it has a very positive impact. In particular, when we have a group of people singing together in a group or choir, there is an added element of bonding that takes place among the group members.

Physical touch is another way to increase oxytocin release. Activities such as massages, a caress, intimate contact, or giving someone a hug will boost oxytocin levels and strengthen feelings of bonding and wellness.

The Impact of Exercise on Your Brain

Do you want to improve your overall brain function in order to have better sharpness and clarity? One of the best ways to do that is to begin a consistent and regular exercise program. Although there are many general health benefits which come from regularly exercising, one of the most notable is the impact of exercise on the brain. I know that any time that I exercise, I certainly feel much better after having done it. Have you ever heard of the term "the runner's high?"

Countless scientific studies have demonstrated how exercise affects the brain in many positive ways:

- The elevated heart rate from exercise results in more oxygen-rich blood being delivered to the brain.

- Hormones are released from your muscles as they flex and contract. Your muscles are your own internal pharmacy, manufacturing chemicals which are secreted into your bloodstream and then picked up by the brain. Performing focused physical activity and movement is what causes this to happen.

- Regular exercise has shown to increase growth in the brain and improve neural development. This is the concept of neuroplasticity, which is the brain's ability to grow and establish new neural connections. When you are working out, not only are you building muscle, you are also building the neurological infrastructure in your brain and body.

- Exercise can reduce the presence of stress hormones such as cortisol, which has the similar effect of taking antidepressants.

In this chapter, by having a better understanding of how the brain works, we have reviewed some actionable habits that we can begin to implement today. These habits will make a positive impact on our brain, and from that, we can begin to experience some improved results in our lives.

The daily practice of gratitude helps us to focus on the good in our lives and kicks off a very powerful chain reaction. Understanding how the chemical oxytocin is produced in our brain, and what effect it has on our well-being, is impactful when we do some of those activities. And finally, we can all find ways to add exercise into our daily routines, which positively supports both our minds and our bodies.

Strive to make these part of a daily practice, and you can begin enjoying the benefits today. If you take a closer look at some of the successful people that you know in your life, you will find that it is highly likely some or all of these strategies are part of their daily practice.

Keeping in mind that success leaves clues, I invite you to consider this question: **When would now be a good time to get started?**

FRED MOSKOWITZ

About Fred Moskowitz: Fred Moskowitz is a bestselling author, investment fund manager, and speaker who is on a personal mission to teach people about the power of investing in alternative asset classes, such as real estate and mortgage notes, showing them the way to diversify their capital into investments that are uncorrelated from Wall Street and the stock markets.

Through his body of work, he is teaching investors the strategies to build passive income and cash flow streams designed to flow into their bank accounts. He's a frequent event speaker and contributor to investment podcasts.

Fred is the author of *The Little Green Book of Note Investing: A Practical Guide for Getting Started with Investing in Mortgage Notes* and contributing author in *1Habit To Thrive in a Post-Covid World.*

Author's Website: *www.FredMoskowitz.com*

Book Series Website: *www.The13StepsToRiches.com*

Gina Bacalski

USING OUR BRAINS

The K-Pop supergroup and global sensation, BTS, is insanely talented, beautiful, hilarious and fun to watch do just about anything. If they've filmed it, chances are I, along with all the other 8 million ARMY's (Fanbase name of BTS), have seen it. One of the things that ARMY's around the globe love to see is how the members of BTS interact with each other, on and off the stage. They really are more like brothers than band members.

They love spending time with each other as much as they love spending time performing for ARMY's. For our viewing pleasure, they have several shows that they film and release regularly. *RUN BTS* is a variety show where we get to watch BTS play games, do challenges, and complete quests with one another. *Bon Voyage* follows the seven-member super group as they go on vacation to various locations around the world. They also have a series of Behind the Scenes documentaries (*Burn the Stage, Break the Silence, Beyond the Star, Bring the Soul*) where we get to watch BTS in their world stadium tours, and what they are doing, and places they go in the locations they hold concerts.

In all of this media, we get to consume, one thing is made abundantly clear. BTS is connected by something stronger than love or music. Countless times, they finish each other's sentences, walk in sync, fold their arms, move chairs, and cross their legs at the same time as at least one or two other members. I have even seen two members of BTS, Namjoon and Jungkook, randomly start singing the same exact snippet of another artist's song at the exact same time, and in harmony (give it a

Google if you're bored). It's gotten to the point where BTS have made a game out of it and several *RUN BTS* episodes now actively try to play some sort of telepathy game. And it works. Every. Single. Time.

The point of all this, is this "Brain thing" that Napoleon Hill is talking about, is real and actually works.

In my own personal life, I have had countless experiences where, randomly, things suddenly appeared in my mind and I have thought of a loved one or someone I feel a connection to and upon further investigation, that loved one was experiencing the thing I "randomly" thought about.

Sometimes, my husband and I take our ability to "read" each other's minds for granted and get annoyed at each other when someone gets something wrong.

My husband and I re-read this chapter in *Think and Grow Rich* in preparation to write this book submission, and he came home from the gym confessing to me that for the first time in his entire life, the thought entered his mind that he wanted to get a tattoo. From a very young age, Jay rejected the idea or thought that he ever wanted a tattoo and even served in a special forces unit in the military but refused to get the squad tattoo that the rest of his team got because he was so sound in his convictions that tattoos weren't for him.

So, when he came home from the gym, he was puzzled as to why he suddenly had these thoughts. But upon further exploration, he was quite certain he had picked up the brain wavelength from fellow gym goers where tattoos are often on display and abundant.

Upon re-reading this chapter, I also remembered the comical scene in the very first *Ghostbusters* movie where Bill Murray's character is doing "telepathy" experiments. In the scene, he has two test subjects hooked up to an electric shock device. As he holds up a card with the back of the card to the test subjects, they must correctly guess the shape that's on the card or receive a mild shock from the device. One of the test subjects is a beautiful blonde female whom Bill Murry's character is flirting with and skewing the results, and only the other test subject, who is male, is receiving any of the electric shocks, even though he was the only one correctly guessing the card shapes.

Besides the connection I have with my husband, the times that this phenomenon has made the biggest impact on me is when I am in dedicated and focused mastermind groups.

Just yesterday, my religious group had a mastermind discussion where a member of the group asked how to talk about her religious beliefs in God with friends or those around her that have left the faith or don't believe as she does, without offending them or feel like she was pressing her beliefs on them. After a few moments of quiet while we contemplated her query, I offered this sentiment: I have put a lot of thought into my personal "brand," so to speak.

There are things that I want everyone to know about me through interacting with me personally or with my social media presence. I want everyone to know I love Jesus, Jay, and BTS. In that order. And that I have a great sense of humor while living my positive, full, and wonderful life. Jesus is a huge part of my life and I talk about Him as quickly as I do BTS or Jay.

Another person in the group agreed with my statement and offered up that someone else's opinion or trigger is not your responsibility to dance around. As long as you are being kind and respectful, don't sensor yourself in talking with those around you with things that mean the most to you.

A few other people gave their thoughts on the idea as well and the discussion was a very successful one. Even though the original query wasn't one I had myself, I gained a lot by listening to the collective mind around me.

My business partner and I have had countless sessions where we thought about a problem or concern on our own and within seconds of us sitting down together to talk about it, all the answers come spilling from our mouths, minds, and fingertips almost faster than we can speak or write them down.

Our business, 3DKDrama, where we invite women to come to Korea to have a KDrama experience, including your own personal male lead, started as just that. Come to Korea and have fun pretending to be in a KDrama. We'll film and photograph the interactions and experiences you have with your English-speaking male lead and at the end you get to go home with a KDrama that you were in! Sounds pretty cool, right? We thought so too. But there's more.

As we developed ideas and developed ourselves as leaders among women, we knew something major was missing from our big idea. As we thought about it further, and after many mastermind sessions on the topic, we concluded that not only did these wonderful women get to come and have an incredible experience in Korea with a beautiful male lead, but we wanted them to be able to go back to their homes knowing they were the female lead of their own lives.

Through more mastermind sessions, we developed a program of growth, love, and beauty for these women to grow and love themselves in ways they couldn't in any other construct. When they leave us, they will be empowered to do the things, and take the risks, and live the lives they only dreamed about, and they will have the tools to do so using their divine femininity.

We never would have come up with the program or even had the idea in the first place if we hadn't gotten together to mastermind about it. Now when we are together our minds are so connected that when we tap into "mind stimulation" we are an explosive force for good in the world. And I unabashedly and boldly write that statement and know that it's true in my heart and soul.

This is just a small part of what how using the subconscious mind and The Creative Imagination have done and are doing for me. I wonder what it will do for you!

GINA BACALSKI

About Gina Bacalski: Gina is a Real Estate Agent, licensed since June 2018. Her background is in Early Childhood Education where she received her Child Development Associate from the state of Utah and has an AS from BYU-Idaho. For the past seventeen years, Gina thoroughly enjoyed her experience in the service industry helping families in the gifted community.

In 2019, Gina helped Jon Kovach Jr. in his launch of Champion Circle. She brings her genuine love for people, high attention to detail, and strives to exceed client's expectations to the Real Estate industry.

Gina married the man of her dreams, Jay Bacalski, in San Diego, in 2013. The Bacalski's love entertaining friends and family, going on hikes, and attending movies and plays. When Gina isn't helping her clients navigate the real estate world, she will most often be found dancing and listening to BTS, watching KDramas and writing fantasy, sci-fi and romance novels.

Author's Website: *www.MyChampionCircle.com/Gina-Bacalski*

Book Series Website: *www.The13StepstoRiches.com*

Griselda Beck

UNLEASH THE POWER OF YOUR BRAIN

The brain is the operations and communications center of our humanity. It interprets the information we receive, dispatches information that initiates movement, and controls our behavior. It is the epicenter of our thoughts, emotions, and actions, and it has an incredible capacity to create our highest and best outcomes. So, how can we leverage, optimize, and influence our brain's capacity to achieve our full potential? Let's explore three key areas: health, information diet, and the importance of updating our operating system.

Health: Fueling Our Brains for Focus & Agile Operation

Our brain requires fuel to function at optimal performance levels, and proper nutrition is essential to support focus, memory, and overall cognitive function. **Exercise** is also an important component of a healthy brain, as it increases blood flow, which delivers oxygen and nutrients to the brain. Studies have shown that regular exercise can enhance cognitive function, boost mood, and reduce the risk of cognitive decline.

In addition to exercise, **dietary supplementation and diet/nutrition** support are also important for brain health. Omega-3 fatty acids, for example, have been shown to improve cognitive function, memory, and mood. Vitamin B complex, magnesium, and zinc also play a critical role in brain health. These nutrients support the neurotransmitters that are responsible for regulating mood, sleep, and cognitive function.

Quality sleep is vital for our brains, allowing it to rest, recharge, and process the events of the day. I'm sure you've heard the term "sleep on it" as an action to take when processing a big decision. During sleep, the brain consolidates memories, strengthens neural connections, and flushes out toxins. Without sufficient sleep, our cognitive abilities suffer, affecting our focus, decision-making, mood, and overall performance. It's like trying to operate on outdated software that is prone to crashes and errors. By prioritizing quality sleep as part of our brain health regimen, we ensure that our brain operates at its highest capacity, enabling us to tackle challenges, think creatively, and excel in our endeavors.

Just as a car requires high-quality fuel to run efficiently, our brain requires proper nutrition and exercise to function at its best. By taking care of our physical health, we can optimize our cognitive function and achieve our highest potential.

Information Diet: Nourishing Our Minds with High-Quality Information

The information we consume shapes our thoughts, beliefs, and actions. Our information diet includes the type of media we consume, the people we surround ourselves with, the communities and environments we put ourselves in, and the information we choose to focus on. Just as we must be mindful of what we eat, we must also be intentional about what we consume in terms of information.

We live in a world that bombards us with information, much of which is negative and fear-based. When we consume negative information, it can create stress and anxiety, which can hinder our cognitive function and reduce our ability to focus. On the other hand, when we consume positive and uplifting information, it can boost our mood and enhance our cognitive function.

More importantly, when it comes to manifestation and creating the results you desire in business and in life, surround yourself with content related to your specific goals. For example, if your goal is to create passive income as a real estate investor, start following, reading, and joining groups created for and made up of real estate investors. This supports, with research, specialized knowledge, networking/proximity, masterminding, programming this destination/outcome in your subconscious mind, imagination, auto-suggestion, organized planning (many of which are topics from earlier volumes in this series).

By being intentional about the information we consume, we can nourish our minds with high-quality information that supports our goals and aspirations. We can choose to focus on information that empowers us, inspires us, and motivates us to be our best selves.

Updating Our Operating System: Rewriting Limiting Beliefs as Powerful Truths

Our beliefs shape our thoughts, emotions, and actions. When we hold limiting beliefs, it can hinder our ability to achieve our goals and reach our full potential. Updating our operating system means doing the work on our subconscious mind to understand our limiting beliefs, release them and rewrite them for powerful truths that serve us.

Our subconscious mind operates like a computer program, running on autopilot based on the beliefs we hold. Another way to look at it is as a filter through which we experience each moment in life. When we upgrade our beliefs, we can reprogram our subconscious mind (choosing a new filter of possibility) to support our goals and aspirations.

An example of a limiting belief might be "I'm not good enough." This belief can create self-doubt, anxiety, and fear, which can prevent us from pursuing our dreams. By reframing this belief to "I am capable and worthy of success," we can create a powerful truth that supports our goals and aspirations.

Updating our operating system requires self-reflection and self-awareness. We must be willing to examine our beliefs, identify the ones that are limiting us, and rewrite them for powerful truths that serve us.

Our brain is an amazing machine that can be rewired and reprogrammed to achieve greatness. However, like any operating system, it requires regular updates and maintenance to ensure it is functioning at its best.

Just as a computer can become sluggish and ineffective without updates, our brain can become limited and ineffective without regular "updates" and "reprogramming."

But what does this "updating" actually entail? It involves doing the work on our "subconscious mind" to understand our limiting beliefs and rewrite them for powerful truths that serve us. It also means reframing the way we interpret the world. It's easy to fall into patterns of negative thinking, but by actively seeking out positive perspectives and focusing on the good, we can reprogram our brains to create successful outcomes.

Think of it like updating the software on your computer. When a new version is installed, your computer is faster, more efficient, and better able to handle new tasks. Similarly, when we update our brain's software, we become more effective, more creative, and better equipped to handle challenges.

Take inventory of your current operating system. Are there limiting beliefs holding you back from reaching your full potential? Are there negative patterns of thinking that need to be reprogrammed? Once you identify these areas, you can begin to take action to update your operating system.

Unleash Your Brain's Potential & Create Magic In The Next Ninety Days!

The brain truly is the operations and communications center of our humanity. It is crucial that we prioritize its health and operation. By focusing on our health, information diet, and updating our operating system, we can leverage, optimize, and influence our brain's capacity to create our highest and best outcome. These factors have a significant impact on our brain's interpretation of the world, and ultimately our behavior.

So, I challenge you to take inventory of these three areas in your life and start with one action tomorrow morning that will make a difference ninety days from now. It could be as simple as incorporating a daily exercise routine, choosing to consume positive media, or setting aside time each day for self-reflection and growth.

Remember, it's the small, consistent actions that create lasting change. You have the power to transform your brain's operation and create the life you desire. Watch as your brain's capacity for greatness expands beyond your wildest dreams.

GRISELDA BECK

About Griselda Beck: Griselda Beck, M.B.A. is a powerhouse motivational speaker and coach who combines her executive expertise with transformational leadership, mindset, life coaching, and heart-centered divine feminine energy principles. Griselda empowers women across the globe to step into their power, authenticity, hearts, and sensuality, to create incredible success in their business and freedom in their lives. She creates confident CEOs.

Griselda's clients have experienced success in quitting their 9-5 jobs, tripling their rates, getting their first client, launching their first product, and growing their business in a way that allows them to live the lifestyle and freedom they want. She has been featured as a top expert on FOX, ABC, NBC, CBS, MarketWatch, Telemundo, and named on the Top 10 Business Coaches list by Disrupt Magazine.

Griselda is an executive with over fifteen years of corporate experience, founder of Latina Boss Coach and Beck Consulting Group, and serves as president for the nonprofit organization MANA de North County San Diego. She also volunteers her time teaching empowerment mindset at her local homeless shelter, Operation Hope-North County.

Author's Website: *www.LatinaBossCoach.com*

Book Series Website: *www.The13StepsToRiches.com*

Jeffrey Levine

MAXIMIZE YOUR BRAIN

Your brain is both a broadcasting and receiving system for the vibration of thought. Our brains are capable of picking up vibrations of thought that are being released by other brains. The creative imagination is the receiving set of the brain which receives thoughts released by other brains.

One of the best ways to use the creative imagination is to be still the first ten minutes when you wake up and at different times throughout the day. I have also received intuitive advice while in the shower or driving my car. These thoughts and ideas usually arrive when you are not focused on anything in particular.

The first time my creative intelligence appeared was when my client, whom I'll call Mr. B, came into my office. Mr. B had twin boys who had just graduated from high school and had been accepted to the same Ivy League college. Tuition and fees for each would be $30,000 a year. He wanted me to find a solution, a way to pay the $30,000 a year for each of them, even though he had no savings and was spending more than he made. It looked pretty impossible to me.

For many weeks, the solution eluded me, though it was constantly on my mind. Then, one Saturday morning, I was alone in my office. There was nobody in the building except me. I wasn't trying to figure out the issue; as a matter of fact, I was dealing with something else when the solution hit me. It came from the universe, and there was no way with the analytical brain I would have been given the same answer. When I least expected it and had nearly resigned myself to the fact there was no solution to Mr. B's dilemma, the answer hit me. I had stopped trying to figure out how to make it happen, though his goal still weighed on my mind. In total amazement to both of us, the solution made itself known.

Another challenging experience appeared when a different client, Mr. W, created money from thin air. He needed $35,000 to pay off a credit card that he was unable to pay on a monthly basis. The rate was 24%. In addition, Mr. W had no cash and was living beyond his means. I had reviewed his finances and situation and had no answer for him. I was really challenged and didn't know what to say to him. The situation was always on my mind, until finally, one day while I was taking a shower, the answer came to me. It came totally off the radar, and I would never have thought of it using my analytical mind.

Mr. W had a pension plan through work. He wanted to take a distribution and pay taxes on the money but would have to pay an extra 10% penalty because he would be taking the distribution before he was 59 1/2 years of age. That would mean he would have to take out approximately $55,000 to net $35,000. That didn't make sense. Why not take a loan instead of a distribution? My solution made more sense because the interest rate would be very low, and he wouldn't have to pay taxes and a penalty. At the same time, he would be paying himself back rather than the credit card company.

The solution worked out really well. It came totally off the radar. It had never occurred to Mr. W, and he couldn't understand how I came up with the idea. But he liked the solution that came to me at the most unexpected time and place.

Our job is not to figure out how, but rather "the what" of our dreams. Once we figure what we want and understand the laws of the universe, we turn everything over to the higher laws that will figure out the how and send it our way. This will not come into our conscious mind from our efforts or willpower. Instead, the ideas will come seemingly out of left field from things we do not expect or ways we are just not aware of.

As another example, I was ready for a new car because my lease was coming due at the end of the year. The car I really wanted was a silver C 300 Mercedes Benz. I was very clear about the exterior and interior colors I wanted. I test drove the specific model and smelled the scent of the new car. I could see myself driving it from the show room. I knew the payment amount and knew what the insurance would cost me. However, realizing that I had an almost two-year-old grandson and another one on the way, buying an SUV made more sense because it was bigger and safer.

The solution also came unexpectedly. I was talking with my son, who informed me that when I took my grandson anywhere, I had to take his car, an SUV, because it was the safest car on the road. Because of that stipulation, I no longer had a need for an SUV. When I went to the dealership, they offered me a great deal on a new C 300. That just happened to be the only car available in the exact color I wanted.

On one Friday after Thanksgiving, I was driving to my local post office to send out a package. Usually, the road past the post office is closed. That day, though, it was open. Since I am a Curious George type, I drove on the new road where I saw houses starting to be built. Because of the view, I walked into the sales office and, to my surprise, was offered a lot that had been canceled ten minutes prior. That person had already paid for it, so I was given an amazing deal. Also, because I was only the third buyer of the new homes, I was given a pre-construction price.

As I mentioned earlier, our job is not to figure out the how but rather the what of our dreams. Once we figure out what we want and understand the laws of the universe, we turn it over to the higher laws that will figure out how and send it our way. As I shared with my different stories, the solutions to my challenges came to me in different ways. However, the answers came off the radar and in ways that I could never figure out myself.

Trust the power of your brain, and you'll be surprised with answers and solutions that you probably could never figure out on your own.

JEFFREY LEVINE

About Jeffrey Levine: Jeffrey is a highly skilled tax planner and business strategist, as well as a published author and sought-after speaker. He's been featured in national magazines, on the cover of *Influential People Magazine*, and is a frequent featured expert on radio, talk shows, and documentaries. Jeffrey attended the prestigious Albany Academy for high school and then went on to the University of Hartford in Connecticut, the University of Mississippi Law School, and Boston University School of Law, and earned an L.L.M. in taxation. His accolades include features in *Kiplinger* and *Family Circle Magazine*, as well as a dedicated commentator for Channel 6 and 13 news shows, a contributor for the *Albany Business Review*, and an announcer for WGY Radio.

Jeffrey has accumulated more than thirty years of experience as a tax attorney and certified financial planner and has given in excess of 500 speeches nationally. Levine is the executive producer and cast member in the documentary *Beyond the Secret: The Awakening*.

Levine's most current work, *Consistent Profitable Growth Map*, is a step-by-step workbook outlining easy-to-follow steps to convert consistent revenue growth to any business platform.

Author's Website: *www.Strategies.org*

Book Series Website: *www.The13StepsToRiches.com*

Lacy & Adam Platt

CRAZY BRAIN & THE AMAZING POWER OF THE BRAIN

Crazy Brain

Have you ever experienced what some call, "Crazy Brain?" Basically, it is the concept that you can't focus your mind; it seems like it is running at 100 miles an hour and you feel like you can't make a decision, no matter what the situation. There was a point in my life when I felt like my brain couldn't comprehend anything beyond the everyday things that I needed to get done.

I also referred to this as "Mom Brain" or when I went into something I refer to as "Survival Mode." This happened just after giving birth to my twins. I was so hyper focused on their well-being and taking care of them that I couldn't even think about anything else. I still had three other kids to raise, yet I felt like my brain couldn't concentrate on anything that they might need. It took almost a year to come out of "Survival Mode" and to realize that there was more to focus on than just the twins.

It was about that time in my life when I discovered personal development. Thankfully, this really helped me to understand how my brain work and why I was making the choices that I was. I discovered that my brain was a lot more powerful than I had ever imagined. To really dive deep into personal development, you must realize that your brain functions on autopilot most of the time. This means that everyday decisions just kind of run through a filter in your mind where you already know the answers to them, and you just keep making the same ones over and over again.

Once I discovered personal development, I learned that I needed to change that Autopilot brain into a higher-functioning version. It was like my whole world shifted! For the first time, I realized how many of my old patterns and daily habits were not helping me.

As this is the twelfth step in the *13 Steps to Riches* series, I hope that you have already heard about and are practicing using your brain in a different way than you ever have before. But let's just assume you're just beginning. There is power in keeping yourself in a state of constant and continuous learning. So, let's go to that place!

Your brain has two different parts. This can be explained in many ways, but, to put it simply, one side is all about language and the other side is all about visual. When you have thoughts or information that enter your brain, it immediately gets transferred to the portion of the brain in charge of processing it.

One of the first steps I teach people is to engage both sections of their brain several times a day—most of the time, we don't do this. When you are aware that you need to process things using both sides of your brain, you can really harness the full power of your brain. If you were working towards something and you simply focus on the language side, you will be successful over time; however, if you were to take that same goal and focus both sides of your brain, you would achieve that goal so much faster!

This is why I say that awareness is everything: When you are in autopilot, you are just making your way through the day not really noticing anything around you. The words and visuals are just passing through your brain, not really causing any action from you. But if you are aware of the fact that you are not using both sides of your brain to comprehend and understanding everything that comes to you, it shifts the way you respond to the world.

This should be very exciting, because it's simply just a choice! A choice to choose to do things differently than you've ever done them before! I love Einstein's quote about doing something over and over while expecting a different result, which is clearly the definition of insanity! Einstein also said, "If you do what you've always done, you'll get what you've always got." If you think about these two quotes, they're saying the exact same thing!

What level of your brain are you using? Most of us simply let things happen to us and allow our subconscious autopilot brain to react the way it's always reacted without considering the option of choosing to respond differently. Choose something different!

~ Lacey Platt

The Amazing Power of the Brain

The brain is an extraordinary tool to help you achieve what you want in life. Everything is created in the brain first before it is materialized in the world. The thing is, I thought my brain was broken for many years.

When I was younger, I had a learning disability in school. I struggled to read, spell, and write. I thought I was stupid and wouldn't be able to achieve much in life. This caused problems with my self-esteem, my confidence, and, of course, my overall progression as a person. Luckily for me, things started to click much better when I got into high school. I was a better student, but a lot of damage was already done. However, in retrospect, I know my brain was not broken. Sure, I struggled to learn, but my brain still worked and my brain helped me achieve where I am today.

The thing about the brain is that it's not just about smarts and how much you can learn from a book. I'm not discounting that kind of learning, but the real power of the human brain is found in the person's desire to want more in life. I have been able to achieve the things I have desired and wanted in life and much of that started in the brain.

So, let's break this down into what I am talking about. Once you have a desire for something, you use three different parts of your brain to make it a reality. The three parts are the subconscious mind, the imagination, and autosuggestion. Those three parts are covered more extensively in other books in this series, so I won't go into a lot of detain in each one, but I want to touch on how this all works. You have a desire for something and that gets filed away in your subconscious—kind of like when you are interested in buying a certain type of car and suddenly you start seeing that car and probably even the color all over the place.

That's your subconscious putting the desire not only into your mind but into the universe. Then you start to imagine yourself in that car; as you visualize it, you are putting that autosuggestion into the brain. Now, pump positive feelings into the imagination and autosuggestion and you are telling yourself and the universe you are ready for that car or whatever it is you want in your life.

I have seen this work, even with my so called "broken brain," time and time again. I used this process to attract my wife to me; I used this to get jobs I wanted and the amount of pay I expected from those jobs. I used it when I was thirteen to win a bike I really wanted in a raffle from a work party I was at. All these instances came about because I had a desire for these things and saw myself having them—I infused faith into these desires.

Sure, I had to work for some of them as well, which is where imagination came into play. Once you activate the desire and fuse it with positive emotions and autosuggestion, your imagination will bring things through your subconscious mind and how you can achieve or have what you desire. I had to convince my wife that I was the right guy—that took effort and time—but seeing myself with her gave me ideas of what that looked like and how to treat her like the queen that she is and win her over.

This is how the law of attraction works. You must start with that desire, create what you want in the mind, and then your imagination will help you come up with the ideas and steps to achieve what you want.

So, even though I thought my brain was broken when I was younger, it was still helping me get what I wanted and where I am today. I love what Napoleon Hill said about the brain in *Think and Grow Rich*. Napoleon Hill said, "Perhaps we shall learn, as we pass through this age, that the "other self" is more powerful than the physical self we see when we look into the mirror."

All things are possible when you harness the power of the brain and create the life you always wanted.

~ Adam Platt

LACEY & ADAM PLATT

About Lacey Platt: Lacey is an energetic, fun loving, super mom of five! She is an Achievement Coach, Speaker and new Bestselling Author who enjoys helping everyone she can by getting to know what their needs are and then loving on them in every way that she can. Her ripple effect and impact has touched the lives of so many and continues to reach more lives every single day. Allow Lacey to help you achieve your goals with proven techniques she has created and perfected over years of coaching. Her and her husband have built an amazing coaching business called Arise to Connect serving people all around the world.

About Adam Platt: Adam is an Achievement Coach, Speaker, Trainer, Podcast Host and now a Bestselling Author. Adam loves to help people overcome the things stopping them from having the life they really want. Adam owns and operates Arise to Connect. Adam believes that connection with yourself, others, and your higher power are the keys to achievement and greater success in life. He is impacting thousands of people's lives with his message and coaching. He lives in Utah with his five daughters and dog, Max.

Author's Website: *www.AriseToConnect.com*

Book Series Website: *www.The13StepsToRiches.com*

Louisa Jovanovich

THE POWER OF THE SUBCONSCIOUS MIND

We are driven by subconscious minds to believe the stories we tell the world, rarely realizing they are just bits and pieces of reality that we put together as truth. We allow our subconscious to dictate our beliefs of what is real and what is not. Once we realize this, it opens up amazing new possibilities and opportunities. This is my story of realization.

I'm sitting in my bed writing this, thinking about my life. I am 47 years old. I am a mother of two teenagers; I am a hairdresser; I am a transformational life coach; I am single, and I have gotten very clear on what I like and what I do not like in life. I spend a lot of time at the salon connecting with beautiful clients doing hair and just as much time at home on zoom calls learning and teaching.

One of the things I recently rediscovered is hot yoga. I first got into hot yoga when I was living in Florida, during a pivotal moment in my life. I seem to be there again, living at the edge, breaking free.

I think I'm beginning to truly see and understand my self-worth. I've been working on this as a concept for years. I am beginning to embody self-love. I used to believe I wanted to be with someone who would be willing to sing their love for me from the rooftops. I came to realize I actually needed to do that singing for myself. A daily practice of journaling is helping me get closer to that goal.

My life has been a story of childlike wonder and curiosity. When I listen to my deep sense of knowing, I can tell I'm always being drawn to finding new and incredible things, both about myself and about everyone around me. Not in the sense of ego, but in the sense of self-love. This creates an opportunity to give generously because I'm so full of joy and fulfillment.

The brain is like a filing cabinet: It pulls memories out of the files of the subconscious. Your subconscious is not emotional. It's very "matter of fact" and it doesn't care about anything other than executing what you ask of it. I've intentionally become very clear and specific about what I put into my subconscious and the impact has been significant.

Before I put a file in a drawer of the subconscious, I ask questions like, "Who am I and does this fit with who I want to be? Is this file in alignment with what I want? Does this file help me get to who I want to be?"

I remember that, as a child, I felt very curious. I constantly watched people. I took in what was happening around me like a sponge. I listened like a hawk to what I felt I needed to learn.

I had some fears, too—actually, I had some big fears. I remember being afraid of things I didn't understand. I thought I could get past my fears by learning more. If I could just learn enough, those fears would go away. For example, I had fears about money. I felt if I learned enough about money and how to invest, I would be "safe." I thought I could "manage" my fears of money through learning. I had fears around my body and my weight. I felt desirable because I was thin. I worried that if I ever got bigger, I would stop being desirable. I managed this fear through strict discipline of myself.

I was attempting to keep control of my life by keeping my outside world safe and predictable. Well, as we know, the reality is that life doesn't work that way.

What do I want? I used to believe I was supposed to want to get married, to buy a house, have children, save money, and live a safe, predictable, happy life. I believed I had to get married at "the right age" in order to not miss out on my baby-making years. These were beliefs I was influenced to believe. As you can imagine, these beliefs set me on a clear and precise mission: FIND THE ONE. I was so set on this mission of finding "the one," and I made decisions based primarily on logic: Make sure he had the skills to give me the life I was programmed to believe I wanted.

I ignored the physical reactions our bodies give us to alert us when something is out of alignment. My brain, my heart, my gut were all trying to speak to me about things that weren't sitting well. I didn't care. I had already decided the time was ticking and I had to make a decision. The price of "missing the window" to have children was more important than waiting for the "right man." I said to myself, "No one is perfect." These red flags are just part of life. I wanted the "bigger picture." The house, the family, the security. I was going to have it all.

I told myself to be quiet. I wanted what I wanted and I was going to pay any price to have it. I was willing to be the one to suffer. I surely couldn't expect the person I dragged into my mission to suffer. It was my doing, so I took on all the suffering—or so I thought. I wasn't taking into account creating suffering for him and the children. I couldn't see this when I was in it. It's only in looking back that I see the clarity of the choices I was subconsciously making at the time.

My childhood fears around money and my body were still haunting me. I still felt I hadn't learned enough to keep my money safe and growing, and I was working out every day to stay fit and look good. I had conflicting beliefs around both fears. I believed I needed to be fit and know about money to be safe, but I also felt these were where the world would take advantage of me. I was still missing the mark on freedom.

With effort, I've been able to work through this and find freedom. Do you know what happens when things open up like this? You find clarity and wisdom. You find the ability to take action. It's a powerful place of integrity. I'm no longer reacting to my life and the fears I carried through much of my life. I'm now creating from a place of trust and surrender. I've replaced the old conversations and limiting beliefs in my head. I've consciously put new beliefs, new files, in my subconscious. Now when something comes up and my subconscious goes to pull a file from the filing cabinet, there are new and improved files to pull from.

Are you wondering how to replace the old with the new? Here's how I did it. First, I accepted that what I grew up hearing and believing was not true. It was simply what I had accepted as truth based on what I had been around and chosen to take in. Next, I began practicing daily mantras and meditations to input new thoughts and beliefs. I created so many new files they actually replaced the old ones. I realized the brain is a powerful tool that has the capacity to create, innovate, and achieve great things.

In order to fully harness our brain's potential, it is important to understand how the brain works and how it can be trained to work for us.

One key aspect of the brain is its ability to change and adapt. This is known as neuroplasticity. It means we can shape the structure and function of our brains through our experiences, thoughts, and behaviors. By intentionally practicing positive habits and focusing on a growth mindset, we can literally rewire our brains to become more resilient, creative, and adaptable.

Another important factor in the brain's ability to drive success and achievement is our emotions. Emotions are a natural part of being human. Among other things, they influence our decision making, motivation, and overall well-being. Learning to manage our emotions and cultivate a positive emotional state can help us stay focused and energized, even in face of our fears and challenges.

The brain also benefits from regular exercise. In the same way we need to keep our bodies fit and healthy, we also need to challenge our brain through new experiences and learning opportunities. This includes things like reading, taking on hobbies or skills, or engaging in activities that require critical thinking.

The brain is a powerful tool for achieving success and growth. By understanding how it works and implementing strategies to optimize its function, we can unlock our full potential and achieve our goals.

LOUISA JOVANOVICH

About Louisa Jovanovich: Louisa is the founder of Connect with Source. She is a mindfulness and emotional intelligence coach. She helps identify blindspots and create new beliefs which empower her clients to access a life they have never dreamed possible. She has completed twenty years of personal and transformational growth, including Landmark Forum and Gratitude Training, and is a Clarity Catalyst Certified trainer. She works with entrepreneurs who seek clarity and want to up-level their lives.

Her life experiences and school of hard knocks are what make her a knowledgeable and compassionate leader and enable her to help guide others through the process of looking for answers within in order to find success and breakthrough their limiting beliefs. Her unique coaching techniques help her clients see the truth behind the stories that are keeping them stuck in the reality that they created.

Louisa is a single mother of two teenagers living in LA. Her love and compassion towards others are her superpowers, helping others reclaim their confidence, find their voice, and know their worth.

Author's Website: *ConnectWithSource.com*

Book Series Website: *www.The13StepsToRiches.com*

Lynda Sunshine West

BRAIN WAVES & THOUGHT BROADCASTING

"Every human brain is both a broadcasting and receiving station for the vibration of thought."
~ **Napoleon Hill**

Have you ever finished somebody's sentence? Or, when someone was speaking, did you know exactly what they were going to say next? This happens in situations with people we have known for a long time (family, friends), but it also happens in situations with people that we don't know. What about the time you had an awesome idea for a product? You just knew it would be an awesome product and that you could sell millions.

But time went by and you didn't act upon it and let the idea rest. Then, a year or two later, you saw your idea (this was "my" idea) in the store selling for $23.99. You think, "What? How the heck did they get my idea? I didn't even tell anyone about it."

This happened to my husband and me. We were camping back in 1995 and didn't like the idea of using a BBQ grill that other people had used. It felt unsanitary. When it can be avoided, I won't use other people's "stuff." But we had no other options because that's what was available to us at that time, a community BBQ grill.

We started talking about how there should be a disposable BBQ grill for people who don't want to use a community BBQ grill when camping; it

171

would be for people who are camping out in the wilderness, who aren't cavemen and don't know how to rub two sticks together to create a fire. Campers could carry the BBQ grill in their backpack, cook their yummy s'mores, then put it back into their pack to take out of the wilderness when they're done and dispose of it safely.

Then, six months later, we were in a local store looking around and saw, what? OUR disposable BBQ grill. We invented it a short six months prior. How did they get our idea so fast, create it, then get it into the marketplace?

Yes, we really believed this was the scenario.

But, as I sat down to write this chapter, I Googled to see when the BBQ grill was actually invented (I couldn't Google anything back in 1995 when we had our idea because Google wasn't founded until 1998). It was invented way back in 1976 and launched in 1984 as the *Disposafeuerbarbekuker,* named after the inventor, Gustaf von Feuerlichter.

We had the idea, but someone had it before us—years before us. It was invented by someone many years before the idea came to us. We didn't use the internet to hear about the idea; it came to us while we were camping and experiencing a challenge with our BBQ situation.

Even though this product had already been invented but we hadn't heard of it before, yet we had the idea, does this mean that our brains were transmitting information not only amongst the two of us, but also the person who put the product on the shelf in 1995 when we first saw it? Had that transmission been broadcasting since 1976 when Mr. von Feuerlichter invented it?

I have more questions than answers related to this topic. As a matter of fact, I don't have any answers, just questions.

Questions, though, open our minds, hearts, and souls to dive deeper into what's possible. By asking these questions, has it opened your mind to other things that are happening in your own life? Is it giving you an idea about "what could be," based on what you already know?

What if we were all born with the ability to tap into other people's brain waves, but, as humans, we stopped ourselves when we were young because it was scary or we thought we were crazy or something else? Can we tap back into it? If so, would you want to?

But we don't need to go that far to tap into someone's mind. We don't have to be able to read their mind, but, better yet, we can simply ask them their thoughts (as addressed in Volume 9, *Mastermind*, in the *13 Steps to Riches* series of books). When we bring together our thoughts and share our own ideas, visions, passion, desires, weaknesses, setbacks, and accomplishments, we can achieve so much more (if we are open to hearing and learning from each other).

The brain is fascinating. What's extra cool is that we don't need to know how it operates and how it does its thing. It just does it. How it works and what it does is intangible to us, but it does what it needs to do to keep us going.

What messages are you broadcasting to your fellow human beings? My hope is that my broadcasts are kept in the positive light so as to create a better planet.

LYNDA SUNSHINE WEST

About Lynda Sunshine West: As the Founder and CEO of Action Takers Publishing, Lynda Sunshine West's mission is to empower five million women and men to share their stories with the world to make a greater impact on the planet. She is affectionately known as The Queen of Collaboration.

Lynda Sunshine is a Book Publisher, Speaker, Multiple Times #1 International Bestselling Author, Executive Film Producer, and a Red Carpet Interviewer. At the age of five, she ran away and was gone an entire week. She came home riddled with fears that stopped her from living and, in turn, became a people-pleaser.

At age fifty-one, she decided to face one fear every day for an entire year. In doing so, she gained an exorbitant amount of confidence and now uses what she learned to fulfill her mission. She believes in cooperation and collaboration and loves connecting with like-minded people.

Author's Website: *www.ActionTakersPublishing.com*

Book Series Website: *www.The13StepstoRiches.com*

Maris Segal & Ken Ashby

BRAIN HACKING

Napoleon Hill very clearly expressed the idea of a "brain hack," stating that our thoughts and emotions are the key to unlocking our potential for success. He wrote, "Your brain is the central transmitting station that controls every other part of your body, through the medium of thought." This idea has been confirmed by research in many studies of the brain. By controlling our thoughts and emotions, we can control our actions, and ultimately, the outcome is a "brain hack" of powerful significance.

Science informs us that the brain is the central processor of all our thoughts, feelings, and actions, and it plays a vital role in determining our success or failure in our personal and professional lives. The significance of this is that the brain can be trained and programmed (or reprogrammed) to achieve greatness in each of us. The opportunity is to understand how it works and how to use it to our advantage. As you read on, think about how this applies to your own life.

Neuroplasticity

Our brains have the constant ability to change and adapt in response to new information and experiences. This process known as neuroplasticity means that the structure and function of the brain can be altered through learning and experience. We have a choice in how and what we feed our brain and how we respond to what we feed it.

As a result, we can train our brains to think and behave in ways that support any of our desires in our work and in all of our relationships.

Neuroplasticity allows us to alter the structure and function of our brain to achieve our goals and reach our full potential.

Thoughts & Emotions, the Keys to Success

Research and wisdom teachers agree with the philosophy that our thoughts and emotions are the key to unlocking our potential for success at any age, from youth through adulthood. An ancient Chinese proverb, points to this as well: "Be careful of your thoughts, words, actions, habits, and character—these become your destiny."

So, simply by changing the way we think, we can alter the emotional and behavioral patterns of neural activity in our brain and create new neural pathways that support our desired outcomes. Simply put, this process is like reprogramming a computer. At work, it's typical to update old software and install a revised program to improve technology's performance. The same applies to us mere mortals! Think of your mind as the computer.

To program (or re-program) our brain, we must first understand the power of our subconscious mind. Our subconscious mind is responsible for controlling our habits, beliefs, and attitudes, and it is constantly influencing our thoughts and actions. According to Hill, our subconscious mind is responsible for 95% of our behavior and decisions, and it is influenced by the words and messages we repeatedly feed it.

This means that if we want to change the patterns of our behavior and thoughts, we must first change the messages we give our subconscious mind. Did you know that our brains can only process positive or negative at one time. We have a choice in each moment. It's often easier said than done, choosing to respond positively versus reacting negatively.

Affirmations & Visualization

One of the most powerful tools for reprogramming our brain is "affirmations." Affirmations are positive statements that we repeat to ourselves, and they help us to feel possibilities and change our limiting beliefs to create new neural positive pathways. By repeating affirmations regularly, we can shift our subconscious and align our thoughts and actions with our goals. For example, if we want to increase our self-confidence, we can repeat the affirmation, "I am confident and capable," several times a day, and even post it with a sign in as many places as possible.

Over time, this affirmation will become a new belief in our subconscious mind, and our brain will begin to support this new belief by guiding us towards confident and capable actions. Just like building and strengthening muscles, repetition is key!

Another effective tool for reprogramming our brain is "visualization." Visualization is the process of creating a mental image of what we want to achieve. By visualizing our desires and our goals, and imagining ourselves already living them, we create powerful neural pathways that support our desired outcomes. Whether you are seeking a new, healthy, loving relationship or a new business opportunity, visualization, along with affirmations, supports our belief in ourselves and our abilities, and it activates the parts of the brain responsible for motivation and action.

As partners in love and business, we utilize "affirmations and visualizations" daily in every aspect of our lives, and we coach our clients, from families and executives to sports and entertainment celebrities across public and private sectors, to do the same. Recently, we began repeating a specific desire and goal and each time we said it, we could feel the accomplishment as if it had already happened. We set the affirmation and a "by when" date when we would have a number one bestselling book.

When we began this process and repetition daily, we had not written a single word. After a month, in spite of our doubts, we acted and began writing. We left the fear and doubt behind and chose to embrace a messy and imperfect process. So, 50,000 words later, we submitted a manuscript to an editor.

During the back-and-forth with the editor, we encountered a snag and decided that we would put a hold on the project. The "by when" date for having a bestselling book was months away, and here we were, back to square one. Feeling a bit defeated yet still committed to our vision, our daily affirmations continued, and our visualization now included where we would be and with whom.

About a month later, seemingly out of the blue, an opportunity was presented to us to participate in this thirteen book collaborative series that you are reading today, *13 Steps To Riches*. We said yes to the invitation without knowing where it would lead. Months later, we woke up in the *location* we had *visualized*, on the *by-when-date*, to hearing the official word that we in fact had our first "bestselling book."

We said earlier that it was "seemingly out of the blue." It was not a random coincidence—it was a "brain hack." By using affirmations and visualization, we reprogrammed our subconscious and "manifested" the desired outcome! Our brain had clearly been guiding us in this direction, supported by a "this is possible" belief mindset and empowered imperfect action.

"Brain hacking" methods involve accessing the subconscious through techniques such as visualization, affirmations, or even hypnosis. The central aspect is that our subconscious mind, which operates beneath our conscious awareness, has the ability to powerfully influence and interrupt our thoughts, emotions, and behaviors. These methods reprogram the subconscious mind with new positive beliefs or habits, such as building confidence, overcoming fears, and reducing stress.

While it seems the brain is trying to protect you, it's often your ego that's really limiting you from experiencing new possibilities for relationships and your life.

Reframing Old Stories

One of the tools we use in our work is the process of *"reframing"* old stories that could be keeping you stuck and not supporting your connection to joy and belonging at work and home. *Reframing* is one of four key universal rhythms of relationships that, from our experience and research, reprograms walls into doors, dead-end streets into highways, and opens a portal to infinite possibilities.

The process of *reframing* is surprisingly simple. Think of a traumatic or dramatic experience you had, when you were pre-teen, about which you created a story that diminishes you, holds you back, and keeps you stuck. Write down the situation as clearly as possible without attaching any meaning. Then, write the meaning you created in your mind about the situation. Recognize that the situation, the event itself, had no meaning, and then notice the meaning that you attached to that event.

Now, the "hack:" Create a new story that can support you now. Once you have created this fresh and supportive story of the experience, feed it to your subconscious not once, not twice, but repetitively. This is how the old limiting story has been so deeply engrained in your mind and is the only way to "hack" and reprogram the outdated software of your brain. Using "reframing" to bypass the conscious mind and work directly with the subconscious can be incredibly effective at creating long desired and lasting change.

Applying the "brain hack" to better serve us in our personal and professional lives may be one of the most underutilized personal tools available to us all. Brain "hacking," using the power of our subconscious minds, may be the most exciting field of possibilities for personal growth, self-improvement, and a valuable tool for achieving our goals and reaching our full potential.

Reflections:

1. What brain patterns in your life need "hacking?"

2. Identify negative mind tapes playing in your head that have been running in a loop for months and years and note how they have impacted your life.

3. Create affirmations that can shift your old mindset and begin to use them as a daily practice.

MARIS SEGAL & KEN ASHBY

About Ken Ashby & Maris Segal: From Mindset to Marketing, Ken Ashby and Maris Segal, a husband and wife dynamic duo, have spent the last thirty-plus years bringing an innovative, collaborative voice to issues, causes, and brands. As entrepreneurs, activists, business strategists, executive producers, coaches, authors, speakers, and trainers, Ken and Maris work with the public and private sectors from boardrooms and classrooms to the world stage. They are known for creating high-touch experiences that unite diverse populations across a broad spectrum of business, policy, and social issues.

Their leadership expertise in Business Relationship Marketing, Organizational Change and Cultural Inclusion, Personal Growth, Project Management, Public Affairs, and Philanthropy Strategies has been called upon by companies and their agencies. Their experience includes: consumer and financial brands, Olympic organizers, Super Bowls, America's 400th Anniversary, Harvard Kennedy School, Archdiocese of LA and NY Papal visit planners, the White House and celebrities across the arts, entertainment, sports, and culinary genres. With Ken's expertise as an award-winning singer-songwriter, they launched ONE SONG, a songwriting workshop series designed to unleash creativity in individuals and teams.

Their **DRIVE** method: **D**esire, **R**elationships, **I**ntention, **V**ision and **E**mpowerment sits at the core of their companies Prosody Creative Services, ONE SONG, and Segal Leadership Global to set a path for every client to Build High Performing Businesses and Elevate Personal and Professional Leadership for Maximum Impact and a 360-degree Thriving Life!

Author's Website: *www.SegalLeadershipGlobal.com*

Book Series Website: *www.The13StepsToRiches.com*

Mel Mason

BROADCASTING INWARD

Align the Conscious & Subconscious for High-Frequency Vibrations

We've discussed the power of emitting high-rate vibrations, but there is also power in becoming aware of what we are receiving. One reason so many people struggle with achieving desirable results is because they are unaware of the messages they are implanting into their minds. How does this happen?

According to Napoleon Hill, *broadcasting* is the supplanting of a conscious or unconscious belief onto the subconscious mind. When combined with a strong emotion, thoughts turn into beliefs embedded into our subconscious mind. The tricky part of the process is it can be conscious or unconscious. If there is a misalignment between our thinking and our emotions, the broadcast could impact our psyche negatively and lower the frequency, or rate, of our vibrations.

Most people can easily conjure up positive thoughts to broadcast inward, but many struggle with the emotional piece of broadcasting. Without a strong emotion, positive or negative, broadcasting does not occur. Some people will attempt to force emotions by using drugs or using logic.

These strategies might work in the short term, but in the long term, they fail because feelings can't be forced. Anyone who has struggled with anxiety or depression can confirm forcing oneself to feel happy doesn't work. Similarly, a person who uses caffeine to pump up for work will not broadcast the belief, *I love my job*, into their subconscious.

As forcing emotions doesn't work in broadcasting, denying emotions does not prevent broadcasting. When we suppress or deny a feeling, the feeling does not go away. Broadcasting occurs consciously and subconsciously. Take trauma, for example... When someone experiences trauma, they may suppress uncomfortable emotions and tell themselves (and others), "I'm fine."

But ignoring the emotions does not prevent broadcasting. The strong emotions and thoughts brought on by a traumatic event broadcast in the mind even when we try to deny it. When broadcasting happens subconsciously, it may take substantial self-work to uncover, and then untangle, negative beliefs.

It might seem we are at the mercy of our emotions to broadcast whatever the world forces upon us. But this is not the case. Just because we cannot control our emotions, doesn't mean our emotions control us. Emotions only need to be acknowledged so broadcasting may occur consciously.

The mind is like a radio, able to pick up different broadcasts in the ether, and then project frequencies outward. When we are aware of our emotions and our thoughts, we broadcast knowingly, with understanding and compassion for ourselves when we struggle. In doing so, the vibrations we emit are clearer and at a higher frequency. When there is less conflicting noise within us, we reflect less conflict out into the world.

So, how do we become better broadcasters and send out clear, high-frequency vibrations?

First, we let our emotions in—not to overwhelm us, but to be heard. Forcing, ignoring, or suppressing emotions creates static and conflict between the conscious and subconscious mind. Static can lead to more frustration and less alignment between our conscious and subconscious mind. By acknowledging our emotions—positive and negative, uplifting and painful, we clear away the static.

When I first explain broadcasting to clients, they often ask what they can do to remove static. Before adding to their routines, I steer them first

182

toward the idea of removing interference. We are often best served when we can declutter the myriad of conflicting internal beliefs. If we have a limiting belief, adding a bunch of limitless beliefs doesn't necessarily help. Instead, removing or dissolving our limiting beliefs creates space for the positive parts of ourselves to shine brighter.

I do this through the practice of allowing the now. If there are conflicting voices in our minds, being present and anchoring ourselves in what we are feeling and experiencing in the moment helps to clear the static. Allowing the now helps us become honestly aware of our thoughts and emotions, which in turn turns broadcasting into a conscious process.

Consciously broadcasting means our conscious and subconscious mind are aligned and our frequency is clear. If our station is clear, we can focus on raising our vibrations further. My go-to way to do this is to become a happiness seeking missile. As a happiness-seeking missile, I seek out opportunities and challenges that increase my happiness. It might sound indulgent, but if we're allowing the now, we bring awareness and introspection into what could seem like binging.

For example, as a happiness-seeking missile, we might treat ourselves to a pricey twelve-course dinner with a friend. With allowing the now, during the experience we can dissect what it is that the expensive meal is really doing for us. Maybe, after months of pinching pennies, we find the indulgence in good food is proof of a deep-seeded belief that we are worthy.

Or perhaps, in allowing the now, we come to find we are most looking forward to sharing the story of the meal with coworkers or a different friend. Uncovering these truths may stir up strong emotions and embed new, positive beliefs into our minds, which increases our vibrations.

Of course, even when we broadcast consciously and vibrate at a high rate, we will still run into challenges. Recently, I vibrated at a high frequency and still had two near-death experiences within forty-eight hours. Last week, I exceeded expectations in my Ph.D. leadership program. For the final assignment, I was required to host and facilitate a two-and-a-half-hour workshop with a minimum attendance of twenty-five people. I managed to enroll over one hundred people in the workshop and had to upgrade my Zoom account to host everyone. The attendance and engagement in the transformational teaching workshop was incredible. As I closed my laptop at the end of the session my hands were shaking, and I had the distinct sensation I was born to be a transformational trainer.

Several fellow Ph.D. candidates were waiting for me at a nearby hangout spot to celebrate, so I brushed my emotions aside, thinking I'd sort through them later. On the drive home, on the same road where I had totaled my truck eighteen months earlier, I hit a patch of black ice and my truck spun out. Suddenly, I was on the side of the road lodged between two Manzanita trees, not more than two yards away from a thousand-foot drop.

"Phew," I thought when the car stopped. The California Highway Patrol officers laughed with me about how close to death I came—if I had been driving ten more miles per hour and hit the same patch of ice, I would be down the cliff-side. But, as it were, there wasn't a scratch on me. The firemen arrived and assessed the road and roadside for hazards. In the clear, they arranged for me to get a ride home, so I didn't have to wait for the tow truck to dislodge my truck from the manzanita trees!

On the short drive home, I brushed aside the near-deadly car crash, and focused on the great result of the workshop. Lurking in the back of my mind though, I sensed static. I had let myself shine bright and it felt right, yet some old broadcasting was interfering with the new.

The next day, I went for a jog, and as I hit my runners' high, a screech came from behind. Adrenaline pumped through my veins, and as I looked back, a work truck was barreling towards me. I lept from the bike lane up onto the curb just in time to avoid getting run over! The truck ran off the road right in front of me! I had stopped running, but my breathing was hard and fast. A second near-miss in forty-eight hours.

"Okay," I thought, "time to allow the now, NOW."

Up ahead, the driver got out of the truck, and took shaky steps away from the car. He was on the phone, no doubt on the line with 911. I thought maybe I should see if he was okay, but I needed to give myself a brief moment. The static in my broadcasting became clear. Giving myself time to be in the now, rather than race ahead to the next task, I heard a tiny voice whispering to me in the static, telling me to turn down my light—I was shining too bright.

Ah. An old, embedded belief. Had I practiced allowing the now post-workshop, I may have recognized sooner my shaky hands were a sign of excitement twinged with anxiety. A part of my psyche was afraid of flying too close to the sun. Now that I was aware of the interference, I could go forward with the understanding I might experience some tension, and I'd be on the lookout for positive broadcasting opportunities.

Using the broadcasting principle, we can all better monitor the messages embedding in our minds. When we master broadcasting, our outward vibrations become clearer. For me, once I cleared out the static, interruptions to my high-rate vibrations lessened—two brushes with death (three if you count the first car crash) is more than enough for one lifetime!

MEL MASON

About Mel Mason: International Bestselling Author Mel Mason is The Clutter Expert, and as a sexual abuse survivor, she grew up depressed, suicidal, and surrounded by clutter. What she realized after coming back from the brink of despair and getting through her own chaos was that the outside is just a mirror of the inside, and if you only address the outside without changing the inside, the clutter keeps coming back.

That set her on a mission to empower people around the world to get free from clutter inside and out, so they can experience happiness and abundance in every area of their lives.

She is the author of *Freedom from Clutter: The Guaranteed, Foolproof, Step-by-Step Process to Remove the Stuff That's Weighing You Down.*

Author's Website: *www.FreeGiftFromMel.com*

Book Series Website: *www.The13StepsToRiches.com*

Michael D. Butler

IF I ONLY HAD A BRAIN

"If I Only Had a Brain."
~ **Scarecrow**

The Young Brain – Key to the Future

Did you receive adequate brain stimulation as a child? Did someone read to you? Did you have a tutor? Did you have learning disabilities? Were you in advanced placement classes? Were you breastfed?

Give Your Babies the Neuro Edge

When you consider Adam's first job in the Bible, it was beyond College/Doctoral level; it was far beyond what you'd expect a single individual or team of individuals armed with the latest technology to complete. That job was naming all the animals. That's right, name every species, every variation of every animal, every bird, every fish, every type of marine life and sea creature, every type of mammal and four-footed insect, reptile, snake, turtles, etc.

The number of animal species is vast and estimated to be millions. It shows you the tremendous capacity he had to create, remember, and expand his brain function. This story truly shows us what is possible. I hypothesize that brain development should be a life-long pursuit.

Did you know 85% of brain development happens in the first five years of life?

Yes, that's correct. The early years of a child's life are crucial for brain development. Research indicates that a significant portion of neural development occurs during the first few years, shaping the foundation for cognitive, emotional, and social abilities. The experiences and interactions during this period play a vital role in establishing neural connections and pathways.

The best thing parents and caregivers can give young children is attention: Attention by listening, asking questions, and observing. By letting a child talk, think, ask questions, and explore a child is gathering the information necessary to help them navigate the world. Like a computational computer, the hard drive of their brain is working at an ever increasingly rapid rate of speed to gather information, analyze information, and make sense of that information.

Limit screen time for young children. Studies are ongoing and vary and they don't always agree. While it is easy for a busy parent to use digital content like iPads, smartphones, and computers to help babysit our children, it's important to know what children are watching, playing, and doing online. Age appropriate is the big thing here, and parental monitoring is paramount for the child's safety and, of course, ultimate brain development, which will come from real conversations with other real humans.

While it's true that breast milk is widely recognized for its nutritional benefits for infants, and it contains essential nutrients that support overall development, including brain development, it's important to note that scientific research often emphasizes the multifaceted nature of factors influencing brain development. The social side of brain development happens when an infant bonds with the mother during breastfeeding time through eye contact, facial recognition, and non-verbal communication. There are volumes of studies that show children who are breastfed have many neurological advantages.

Americans are Not Reading & How to Fix It

A full 85% of college graduates never buy or read another book after college graduation in the USA. This may stem from 8 or more semesters of buying overpriced textbooks in the college bookstore. Seventy-six percent of books in English are bought and read outside of the USA, and 65-70% of global book consumption is fiction, with 30-35% being non-fiction books, according to Bowker. I'm not sure how we fix it. You can lead a horse to water, but you can't make him drink but you can put salt in his oats. It's not until a person wants to change their learn and change their life that they'll be motivated to do it.

Are You Only Using 10% of Your Brain?

The idea that we only use 10% of our brains is a common misconception. Neuroscientific research has consistently shown that the entire brain is active, and each part has a specific function. While it's true that not all regions of the brain are active simultaneously, there is no evidence to support the claim that we only use a small percentage of our brains.

No doubt our brain is capable of far more than most humans tax it for. Imagine when it comes to learning new languages, playing musical instruments, and solving complex math, and philosophical problems. the human brain has historically exhibited the propensity for genius and beyond. Seeing what an individual brain can accomplish alone makes us only wonder the potential that is possible when many human brains think and act in tandem. Could the collective brain become infinite in that regard?

However, if you're interested in enhancing cognitive abilities and optimizing brain function, here are some evidence-based strategies:

Lifelong Learning

Engage in continuous learning and intellectual stimulation. Acquiring new skills, taking up new hobbies, and pursuing educational activities can help create new neural connections and maintain cognitive flexibility.

Physical Exercise

Regular exercise has been linked to improved cognitive function, including memory, attention, and executive function. Exercise increases blood flow to the brain and promotes the release of neurotransmitters that support cognitive health.

Adequate Sleep

Quality sleep is essential for cognitive function and memory consolidation. Ensure you get enough restorative sleep each night to support overall brain health.

Healthy Diet

Eat a balanced and nutritious diet that includes omega-3 fatty acids, antioxidants, and other essential nutrients. These nutrients support brain health and can contribute to optimal cognitive function.

Mindfulness & Meditation

Practices such as mindfulness meditation have been associated with changes in brain structure and function. Regular meditation can improve attention, reduce stress, and enhance overall well-being.

Social Connections

Maintain strong social connections and engage in meaningful relationships. Social interaction is beneficial for cognitive health and emotional well-being.

Challenging Mental Activities

Engage in activities that challenge your cognitive abilities. This could include puzzles, brain games, or complex problem-solving tasks.

Reduce Stress

Chronic stress can have negative effects on the brain. Adopt stress-management techniques such as deep breathing, yoga, or other relaxation methods to promote brain health.

Stay Hydrated

Proper hydration is crucial for optimal brain function. Dehydration can impair cognitive abilities, so ensure you are drinking enough water throughout the day.

Brain-Boosting Supplements

Some supplements, such as omega-3 fatty acids, vitamin B complex, and antioxidants, may support brain health. Consult with a healthcare professional before adding supplements to your routine.

It's important to note that individual responses to these strategies may vary, and there is no one-size-fits-all approach. Additionally, maintaining overall health and well-being is key to supporting cognitive function. If you have specific concerns or are considering major lifestyle changes, it's advisable to consult with a healthcare professional or a qualified expert in the field.

Preventing Alzheimer's & Dementia

Alzheimer's disease and dementia are significant global health challenges, affecting millions of people. According to the World Health Organization (WHO), around 50 million people worldwide were estimated to be living with dementia in 2020, and this number is expected to nearly triple by 2050.

Preventing Alzheimer's and dementia involves a combination of lifestyle choices, early detection, and management of risk factors. Here are some key strategies:

Healthy Lifestyle

Adopting a healthy lifestyle is crucial. This includes regular physical exercise, a balanced diet rich in fruits and vegetables, and maintaining a healthy weight. Aerobic exercise has been associated with a lower risk of cognitive decline.

Cognitive Stimulation

Engage in mentally stimulating activities, such as reading, solving puzzles, learning new skills, or playing musical instruments. Keeping the brain active may contribute to cognitive resilience.

Heart-Healthy Diet

A diet that is good for the heart is also considered beneficial for the brain. This includes a diet low in saturated fats, trans fats, and cholesterol. The Mediterranean and DASH diets, which emphasize fruits, vegetables, whole grains, and lean proteins, are often recommended.

Social Engagement

Maintain social connections and engage in activities that involve interaction with others. Social engagement has been linked to a lower risk of cognitive decline.

Quality Sleep

Prioritize good sleep hygiene. Poor sleep patterns, including sleep apnea, have been associated with a higher risk of cognitive decline.

Management of Chronic Conditions

Control and manage chronic conditions such as diabetes, hypertension, and high cholesterol. These conditions can impact vascular health, which in turn can affect brain health.

Moderate Alcohol Consumption

If alcohol is consumed, do so in moderation. Excessive alcohol intake can increase the risk of cognitive decline.

Avoid Smoking

Smoking is associated with an increased risk of cognitive decline. Quitting smoking can have multiple health benefits, including reducing the risk of dementia.

Mental Health

Manage stress and prioritize mental health. Chronic stress can contribute to cognitive decline, so adopting stress-reduction techniques is important.

Regular Health Check-ups

Regular health check-ups can help in the early detection and management of any health conditions that could contribute to cognitive decline.

It's important to note that while these strategies may reduce the risk of Alzheimer's and dementia, they don't guarantee prevention.

For the most current and personalized information, it's recommended to consult healthcare professionals and stay informed about ongoing research and developments in the field of neurology and cognitive health.

But the truth is you can improve and preserve your mental function and cognitive ability. Keep your mind young. Talk to young people, travel, read different kinds of books, take different routes to work, and brush your teeth for 30 days with the "other" hand. Say your ABCs backward, count to 1 from 100 backward, and work on crossword puzzles and other exciting games that stimulate the brain. Learn a foreign language, learn some new dance moves, or a new and different musical instrument. This will all go a long way to help rewire the synapsis of your brain and to improve neuroplasticity.

MICHAEL D. BUTLER

About Michael D. Butler: Called the Simon Cowell of Book Publishing, celebrity kingmaker Michael D. Butler is most proud of his four sons and two grandsons. His authors have spoken in fifty countries.

As a global book publisher and speaker, Butler is a recognized authority in the book publishing space, with 794 titles published by authors in sixty-four nations. Helping authors and speakers evolve and create platforms of influence in an ever-changing marketplace.

Founder of 1040Impact.org has rescued 394 girls from human trafficking ages 6-17, caring for them in a safe, loving environment with a full-time staff of twenty-five in Pakistan.

Author's Website: *www.MichaelDButler.com*

Book Series Website: *www.The13StepsToRiches.com*

Michelle Cameron Coulter & Al Coulter

OUR BRAIN ODYSSEY

Navigating the Journey Through Life's Challenges & Resilience in Family, Sports, & Life

Hey there! We're Michelle and Allan, a couple whose journey has been a tapestry woven with threads of resilience, authenticity, and the incredible power within our minds. As we share our story, come along on a journey that spans the Olympic arena, family life, and the unpredictable terrain of business ventures.

Teamwork & the Brain

Michelle: In synchronized swimming, every move needs to be in harmony, just like our family. Our brains are like the choreographers, ensuring that every action is synchronized.

Allan: Our minds are like a team huddle in volleyball. Teamwork, not just in sports but in life, is guided by our brains—the ultimate coaches of our family's dreams.

Our journey is a dance, a collaboration where our minds work together, creating a symphony of teamwork that resonates through the fabric of our lives.

Resilience, Challenges, & the Brain's Triumphs

Michelle: Challenges are a part of life, in sports, family, and business. Our brains are like resilient warriors, equipped to face these challenges head-on. They are the unsung heroes who guide us through storms, turning setbacks into steppingstones.

Allan: Absolutely. Our family's journey is a testament to the bounce-back ability of our brains. It's not about avoiding challenges; it's about facing them together with the mental muscle our minds provide.

Our brains triumph over challenges, not just in the arenas of sports but in the intricate dance of family life and the unpredictable world of business.

Discovering Ourselves with Our Brains

Michelle: Our brains are the architects of self-discovery. In synchronized swimming, it wasn't just about perfect moves; it was a journey of understanding who I am beyond the medals. Our minds are explorers, guiding us through the maze of self-discovery.

Allan: Our brains are like GPS, helping us navigate the twists and turns. The journey of self-discovery is ongoing, a dance where our minds shape the map of our authentic selves.

Our family's journey is a continuous exploration, guided by the incredible capacity of our minds to understand and embrace who we are. And in business, the ups and downs have taught us valuable lessons about adaptability and the strength of our minds in navigating uncertainties.

Overcoming Tough Times in Business & with Our Brains

Michelle: In both sports and business, I faced unique challenges. Dealing with an eating disorder and navigating the unpredictable terrain of business were not just physical battles but mental ones. But our brains, with their resilience and strength, can triumph over personal and professional challenges.

Allan: Michelle's journey taught us that the brain is not just a thinker; it's a fighter. Reaching for one's potential starts with a strong and healthy mind. It's about taking care of oneself, not at any cost, but with love and care.

Our family's narrative is a chapter of vulnerability, strength, and the profound role our brains play in overcoming personal and business battles.

The Brain's Sanctuary for Open Communication in Family & Business

Michelle: Our brains thrive on communication. Our family became a safe space where our brains could share anything, and our minds found the support they needed.

Allan: Open communication is like a secret code for our family's brains. It strengthens our bonds, making us resilient together. It's not just about talking; it's about truly listening and understanding.

In business, open communication became a crucial component. The brain's ability to communicate openly and adapt to changes has been key in facing the challenges of entrepreneurship.

Embracing Our Real Selves with Our Brains in Family & Business

Michelle: As parents, we encourage our kids to embrace the brain's art of being real. Our minds are like artists, creating a masterpiece with our authenticity. Imperfections make us who we are and are not flaws but brushstrokes that add beauty to the artwork.

Allan: Our brains embrace the beauty of being real. It's not about being perfect; it's about being true to ourselves, flaws and all. Authenticity is our family's strength, and our brains are the guardians of that realness.

In business, the art of being real has also played a pivotal role. The brain's capacity to adapt authentically to the ever-changing landscape of entrepreneurship has been a key driver of our ventures.

Connecting Our Epic Adventure to Yours

As you start your own epic adventure, think about the challenges you've faced. Ever felt the strength of your brain guiding you through those moments? The brain's power to turn challenges into opportunities is like a super cool power that connects us all.

Reflect on your journey of discovering yourself. Ever felt the guiding hand of your brain, helping you navigate the twists and turns of understanding who you truly are? The brain's role as a creator of realness is a universal theme that connects us—like heroes sharing their origin stories!

Consider your personal battles. Ever leaned on the strength of your brain to overcome internal struggles? The mind's strength and ability to overcome challenges are like threads that weave through the fabric of the hero experience.

Think about your relationships. Have you ever valued the power of open talks, where the brain's need to connect and share is at the forefront? Open communication as a source of strength is like a superhero tool that strengthens the bonds we share with others—like heroes huddling together to plan their next move!

Lastly, think about the realness in your life. Ever embraced the creativity of your brain, creating a masterpiece with your realness? The brain's ability to embrace imperfections and be true to oneself is like a shared journey that ties us all together—like a league of heroes embracing their unique superpowers!

Cheers to Your Brainy Adventure

As our epic adventure continues, let's raise a toast to your brainy adventure. May your journey be filled with strength, realness, and the continuous discovery of the power within your mind. Your journey awaits, guided by the incredible potential within your brain. Cheers to the brainy adventure called life—you're the superhero of your own story!

MICHELLE CAMERON COULTER & AL COULTER

About Michelle Cameron Coulter: Michelle is an Olympic gold medalist, entrepreneur, mother of four, community leader raising millions of dollars for charities, global inspirational leader, and founder and CEO of Inspiring Possibilities.

About Al Coulter: Al is a two-time Olympian in volleyball, captain of Team Canada, world record holder in matches representing one's country in any sport, with over 735 matches, entrepreneur, father of four, and personal best coach, specializing in relationships, team, and resilience.

Michelle and Al are the embodiment of today's leaders. Strong and empowering, they embraced life's challenges with strength and courage. They bring insight, compassion, depth, and inspiration to the table with multiple world championships, three Olympics, an Olympic gold medal, marriage, and four children.

They are sought-after inspirational leaders. Through their speaking, workshops, and retreats, their gift and passion is to "inspire possibilities" and encourage people to embrace their greatness in a real, authentic, healthy, and vibrant way—creating thriving community, connection, and one's own gold medal results.

Author's Website: *www.MichelleCameronCoulter.com*

Book Series Website: *www.The13StepsToRiches.com*

Dr. Michelle Mras

MUSCLE MEMORY

"The brain is like a muscle. When it is in use, we feel very good."
~ **Carl Sagan**

I have learned that when the mind is idle, it loses track of what it is meant to do. After six months of the 2020 COVID-19 pandemic lockdown, many people witnessed or experienced this phenomenon firsthand. Those who were quarantined in solitude experienced it faster.

What happened? Once the novelty of the extended vacation wore off and we realized we needed personal interactions, we sought distractions from our long, lonely days. Moments blurred into each other. We lost track of minutes, hours, and days. Our time was consumed by surfing the internet, binging shows, stress eating, and other unhealthy habits. Our minds and bodies became idle.

"An idle mind is the devil's playground."
~ Philippians 4:8

The mind is like a muscle. When you stop using it, it begins to atrophy. This happened around the world. We congruently experienced a medical pandemic, which set off a domino effect of depression, despair, obesity, loss of jobs, and, in turn, the atrophy of minds. For those who were wishing for some time off, the global shutdown was a wish granted. From such tales as Aladdin and the Magic Lamp from The Arabian Nights bedtime stories, we learned lessons like, "Be careful what you wish for," and, "You are greater than your situation."

In this case, some discovered new skills, some found other outlets for creativity, and online communities were created. In all the chaos and uncertainty, good did occur. Unfortunately, many never came out of the downward spiral. Some became accustomed to not moving or working. They allowed their apathy to take a grip on their mindset and they have become less of a person from the experience.

I witnessed this decay of society during hundreds of online community calls, trainings, and keynote addresses I have done throughout the pandemic and the years afterward. The decline in hope and the increase of apathy has been significant among many.

I had seen this occur before in my life personally. When I was a military spouse, I moved with my active-duty husband every four years. I had great difficulty obtaining a job with so many frequent moves. Once we had children, the opportunity to work became even more difficult since my husband deployed for weeks at a time, which often left me as a single parent in a foreign county. There were times when I would find myself tearing up or crying from the loss of myself. Every waking moment was scheduled around our young children.

My mind, which was accustomed to high levels of activity, including reading and adult interaction, was not being fed. I felt as if I was losing my mind. I began to dream scenarios that seemed so real that when my husband would return from a deployment, I would accuse him of things that never happened. My mind lost connection to reality. My husband and I discussed my delusional state. He shared with me that he saw the same occur with his mother. She was a teacher, but over the summer, she would get silly. His theory, I agreed, was that we were both highly intelligent women, and when we had nothing to stimulate our brains, we lost touch with reality. It made sense.

How, as a stay-at-home mother, could I keep my mind active while caring for our young children? I became creative with our days: Outings to museums and historical locations, play dates, teaching our children science, learning advanced baking skills, and the like improved my brain function back to normal. Bonus: our children learned at an accelerated rate.

As our children became more independent, my interest gravitated to returning to college, taking courses on cooking, or learning the language of the country we lived. Now that our children are adults, I have expanded my brain repertoire.

During the two-plus-year setback, I experienced in 2014 with my traumatic brain injury, I had to relearn all everyday skills. I believe my neuropathways were more receptive to regrowth because I had challenged my brain for most of my adult life with everything I mentioned above, along with word searches, crosswords, and puzzles. The brain is like a muscle. Once I began to challenge it, my brain remembered how to flex, much like muscle memory.

If we are fortunate, we will reach our retirement years. You have probably seen your parents, a family member, or friend retire. Perhaps, you have reached your retirement? I challenge you to keep your mind and body active. It is important that we keep exercising that "muscle" between our ears every day of our lives.

Upon retirement, keep challenging your mind with new experiences. If you can't travel, visit places within your area. Be a tourist in your town. Play games. Meet new people. Join a mastermind or a group that piques your interest. Every day, complete a word or number puzzle. Keep your mind active and you will reap the benefits of remaining cognitive longer. An active mind has been proven to reduce the onset of Alzheimer's Disease.

Outside of your job, how do you keep your mind actively creating? Add habits to your routine that challenge your mind. Build a strong foundation by adding mental resiliency exercises into your life. The best time to work on increasing your mental acuity is before you start to lose it.

We must remember the lesson that we are greater than our situation or circumstances. Regardless of what you are experiencing, we each have a choice to remain where we are or move through. It is a mindset embraced by those who succeed consistently: Use your mind and your intuition to find your own way through difficult times and keep moving regardless of the pace or whether you know how.

You probably noticed I mentioned intuition as a factor to success. It is quite a major factor in those who embody the *Think and Grow Rich* mentality. The unconscious mind has been studied and part of Eastern religions for centuries. The Western world has recently begun to embrace its importance and recognize that there is more to our minds than what is easily measured. The unconscious mind is referred to as an inner knowing or intuition.

Have you experience the phenomena where a particular person appears in your dreams or you feel the need to reach out to them? Once you do, you discover they were experiencing a stressor and needed you. Perhaps you've had a gut feeling that you want to avoid someone or to take another route to your destination? If you haven't had this kind of experience, perhaps you've heard of one?

The brain is incredible. I believe it has more capabilities than we are willing to admit and that these intuitive feelings or nudges occur constantly within our lives. We don't notice them because our minds are preoccupied with the constant bombardment of information through our electronic devices and busy lives.

I encourage you to find moments of quiet time in your day. Listen for the quiet voice. Your intuition is speaking. Just like your body, your subconscious mind, needs to be exercised in order to work better. Exercise of the subconscious mind is done with meditation. Turn off your mind to allow your subconscious to play a more active role in your life, by creating an opportunity to see beyond what your conscious mind can visualize.

Make it a practice to exercise your brain's capabilities not only through challenging the logical conscious mind, but also the unconscious mind. If you have not experienced meditation, seek meditation guidance online or join a group that will teach you how to quiet your mind. Once you learn the basics, you can create a practice to do it daily.

MICHELLE MRAS

About Michelle Mras, PhD: Michelle is a Global Award-Winning Keynote & TEDx Speaker, Presentation Coach, and Co-Host of two podcasts: Denim & Pearls and Amplifluence. Michelle is the Host of MentalShift on The New Channel (TNC), Philippines. She's a multiple Bestselling Author and Co-Founder of Amplifuence: Amplifying the Influence of Coaches, Authors, & Speakers.

Michelle is a survivor of multiple life challenges to include a Traumatic Brain Injury and Breast Cancer. She guides others to recognize the innate gifts within them, stop apologizing for what they are not and step into who they truly are… Unapologetically.

Author's Website: *www.MichelleMras.com*

Book Series Website: *www.The13StepsToRiches.com*

Mickey Stewart

HIDING IN PLAIN SIGHT

When he was thirteen years old, our son Cameron got his very own copy of *Think and Grow Rich*. We immediately started reading it together, forming our little book club of two. The very next day, as we walked home from a concert, the fresh belief that abundance was all around him was dancing in his brain.

The High Street was busy with concertgoers and others out for a Saturday night. I walked right past something, but Cameron saw it. There, at the side of the street, was a crisp £20 note. It was like it happened on cue, just as he had read the day before in the book's introduction, *"When one is truly ready for a thing, it puts in an appearance."* He was on the lookout for abundance and sure enough, it showed itself to him, while hidden in plain sight to everyone else who walked by.

What makes one person see something while it appears almost invisible to others? Our RAS, the reticular activating system, plays a big role. If the brain is *"the broadcasting and receiving station for thought,"* as Napoleon Hill stated, then the RAS is like the brain's antenna—the part that acts as a filter, to keep a look out for what we're focusing on and what we want. Sometimes that even means drawing on the thought frequencies of other people.

"Every human brain is capable of "picking up" thought impulses which originate in the brain of others."
~ Dr. Nikola Tesla

I read and re-read Napoleon Hill's words and my mind flooded with countless personal stories of evidence that this was true. Hill believed our conscious mind receives stimuli from four sources: 1) Infinite Intelligence, 2) one's own subconscious mind, 3) the "highly energized" conscious mind of another person, and 4) the subconscious storehouse of another person.

Come with me as we delve into the third source, receiving stimuli from the conscious mind of another, and as I retrace the steps of how I was set on a path as if programmed like a human Satellite navigation device by the "highly energized" thoughts from someone else's conscious mind and sent on a fun, unexpected journey through the streets of historic Edinburgh.

In the Spring of 1995, my boyfriend (now husband), Mark, and I were having a day out in Edinburgh. I had only been living in Scotland for a couple of weeks and was excited to explore all the wonderful clothing shops of this amazing city. I knew Mark didn't fancy looking in one ladies' clothing shop after another, so we decided to split up for a few hours of solo shopping.

Edinburgh was a magical place to me (and still is after living in Scotland for over two decades), but in the early years, it was extra-magical. It felt like the world was my oyster, and I loved looking at all the shops, both new and old. I had every intention of looking for clothes that day, but after an hour or so of poking my head into a few stores, I decided I wasn't in the mood for trying on clothes, so I ended up at a bookstore.

In my opinion, the Waterstones bookstore on Princess Street is one of the best in the world, not just because of the wide selection of material but because of the grand staircases that lead to its many levels—making it feel special, like it's a special home to house special books. I could spend hours in a bookstore!

This particular day, I went straight to the Music section, which was located up a few levels next to a large pillar, with the shelves appearing to span from the floor to the high ceilings. In retrospect, they were possibly just a regular height, but everything here seemed grander to me.

I think we see things with greater appreciation, and with our senses in hyperdrive, when we're in awe. I did feel like I was seeing my surroundings differently from the people around me. I was in picturesque Edinburgh, walking through a glorious myriad of natural treasures and man-made history—so beautiful in my bubble of bliss—that I wished everyone else could see it through my eyes at that moment.

I scanned the tall, dark, wooden bookcase from top to bottom, but my eyes were immediately drawn to the very bottom shelf. Something was different about the bottom shelf. Something was causing the books to not quite line up as perfectly. As I bent down to investigate, I could see a book had been shoved behind the others. Why would someone try to hide a book in a bookstore? My curiosity kicked in, and I reached down to pull the book from its hiding place.

My fingers wrapped themselves around the small book, and I smiled to myself as I read the words "Ireland's Musical Instrument Makers: Who They Are and Where to Find Them" by Joyce Pye. I couldn't believe my luck. I had been researching Bodhrán drum making and was so excited to find this gem of a book that wasn't just a directory of makers but filled with wonderful information on instrument making. *"Wait until I show Mark!"* was my immediate thought.

It was almost painful to have to wait until our pre-arranged meeting time. This was before the days of iPhones, so I had no way of contacting Mark to say I wanted to meet earlier. It doesn't take much to excite me, so I was like a kid on Christmas morning. I wanted to learn everything there was to know about making bodhráns with the idea of someday crafting them, but it was still a pipe dream at this point.

Princess Street was bustling as usual, filled with tourists, buskers, businesspeople, locals, and homeless people begging for change. *"You're not going to believe what I found!"* were the words that spilled out of me like an eruption when I met Mark under the towering, 200-foot monument to Scottish author Sir Walter Scott, built in the 1840s.

I didn't know if I was reading his expression correctly because I could see a slight look of disappointment come across his face. I don't think I even waited for him to respond before I started digging my find from its bag. As I did, my first impression of his facial read was confirmed when he saw the book. I was so excited to show it to him! Why wasn't he sharing in my enthusiasm? I couldn't understand.

Mark proceeded to tell me that he got me something and was really excited to give it to me as well. Out of his bag he pulled the EXACT same little book: "Ireland's Musical Instrument Makers." He found it in the same Princess Street Waterstones bookstore as me but saw another copy of it and thought, *"If she comes in here and sees it, she'll buy it too, so I better hide it."* So, he took the extra copy from its shelf and shoved it behind the books on the very bottom shelf so I wouldn't find it.

"Thought manifests itself as electrical energy within the human brain. Only highly intensified or "energized" thought impulses are transmitted from one brain to another through this mysterious and still not understood process."

Napoleon Hill could tell me this in *Think and Grow Rich*, but often it's not until we have our own personal experiences of this happening that we truly believe it. I mean, I had EVERY intention of coming away from Edinburgh with some sassy new clothes and did not plan to go to a bookstore.

Mark and I didn't have any prior discussions about looking for instrument-making books or anything of the kind, but without my awareness, my RAS antenna picked up on his thoughts—just as radio waves are sent from a radio station and then converted to mechanical vibrations, so we can hear the sound waves come out of the speaker of our car stereo.

I believe it was Mark's own excitement about buying me a gift he knew I would love that energized his thought and planted it in my brain, making me completely change the course of my day. Whether it's "I DON'T want this thing to happen" or "I WANT this thing to happen," the electrical energy that Hill mentioned is focused on the THING—not whether you want it or don't want it. For example, if I were to say "DO NOT imagine a black Labrador walking down the street carrying a small monkey on its back," what happens? You immediately start thinking about a black Labrador walking down the street carrying a small monkey on its back, right?

> *"What you think you become.*
> *What you feel you attract.*
> *What you imagine you create. "*
> ~ Buddha

So, what have these above experiences taught me? That, if I wake up each morning with a fresh belief that abundance is all around me, I'm guaranteed to discover hidden gems that may very well be invisible to the plain sight of others.

And, if you were wondering if we ever made drums? After years of research, Mark and I started our own bodhrán manufacturing business, Cape Breton Bodhráns, and our drums went on to be played by musicians throughout Canada, the United States, Scotland, Mexico, and Australia.

MICKEY STEWART

About Mickey Stewart: Born in Cape Breton, Canada, Mickey Stewart is a musician, coach, and author who has been a player and instructor of the snare drum and bodhrán for forty years.

Responsible for heading up the drum program at Ardvreck School in Perthshire, Scotland, since 2002, Mickey is in high demand to teach throughout the U.K. and North America.

Creator and founder of BodhránExpert.com, her YouTube videos have received more than two million views from students and fans from every country throughout the world.

Over the past eight years, she's been involved in the TV and film industry as a supporting artist. Even more recently, she's begun following her newest passion, which is teaching others how to share their talents with the world.

Stewart lives in Crieff, Scotland, with her husband of twenty-six years, Scottish musician and composer Mark Stewart, along with their eighteen-year-old son, Cameron, who is also a piper.

Author's Website: *www.MickeyStewart.com*

Book Series Website: *www.The13StepsToRiches.com*

Natalie Susi

THE RIPPLE EFFECT

In the book, *Think and Grow Rich*, Napoleon Hill devotes an entire chapter to the power of the brain and the importance of developing a "positive mental attitude." According to Hill, the human brain is the most powerful tool we possess, and our thoughts have the ultimate power to shape our reality.

Hill argues that success in any field, whether it be business, athletics, or the arts, begins with the mindset of the individual. He notes that successful people share a common trait: they all possess a positive mental attitude. This means that they approach challenges and setbacks with a mindset of resilience and determination, rather than negativity and defeatism.

To cultivate a positive mental attitude, Hill suggests several key strategies. The first is to control one's thoughts and emotions. He notes that the brain is like a muscle, and just as we can train our muscles to become stronger, we can also train our brains to become more positive and resilient.

Our brain is like a broadcasting and receiving station, affecting every second, minute, and hour of our lives. We must develop the discipline to monitor our thoughts and emotions and consciously choose to focus on positive thoughts and emotions, rather than negative ones.

As a personal and professional development coach, the first step in working with my clients is to help them uproot and uncover their triggers, patterns, and stuck points. I explain that our thoughts create our beliefs, and our beliefs become the stories that we tell on repeat. I ask them to imagine their thoughts are like a well-traveled road in their brain and we call these roads, "neuropathways."

Every time we play into those old beliefs and tell those old stories, it is like we are driving on this same old road over and over again. We are familiar with every pothole and every turn. We know how to drive down that road without even thinking about it. Humans choose the well-traveled road even if it's not fun, not pretty, or not leading to a desirable destination because it's predictable which makes us feel safe and comfortable.

The act of choosing your thoughts and picking the ones that are better for you is simple, but it's not always easy. It is a daily practice. It is a daily choice of saying to yourself, "I'm going to choose to drive down the road that I'm not as familiar with. I'm going to choose to be open to a different direction, a different view, a different destination. I am going to choose to live in faith instead of fear."

Our feelings and emotions also have the power to affirm our imagination and creativity. If we are excited to act on a thought, then we will move towards it freely and without resistance. However, if we have a negative attitude towards a thought, it'll be much harder to commit and finish. Who knew that our feelings towards our daily thoughts would be either the steppingstone to success or result in a snowball effect obliterating one's desires?

This is what allows our thoughts and desires to all come together by utilizing our subconscious mind from the thoughts we transmit, our creative imagination from the thoughts we receive from others, and our autosuggestion that allows us to become crystal clear on what our desire is and how we feel about it. Once you get crystal clear on what you are manifesting or calling in, it will flow effortlessly into your life.

Ultimately, in this life, the most powerful forces are unseen, especially the greatest force of them all: the intangible force of thought. My hope is that you have grasped the importance of acknowledging your inner thoughts, feelings, and emotions. I never knew the severity of negative or impulsive thoughts until I learned about the dynamics of the subconscious mind. When you focus on strengthening your subconscious mind and the energy you allow into your brain, it'll help you manifest and call in your desires much quicker.

Instead of pondering over the tangible forces of life such as a salary, a job promotion, or conflicts that you have zero control over, it is better to transfer that effort into your own well-being. How are your everyday thoughts? What kind of conscious conversations are taking place around the areas of your life that you seeking growth and evolvement? Are you dwelling more on the materialistic aspects of the world, or are you spending more time understanding your emotional wants and needs?

The unseen may be intimidating, but it is the power of faith that outweighs fear. After many years of battling my own mind and inner consciousness, and years of learning the ways the brain functions, I can now say that I move through obstacles much quicker than I did 10 years ago. It is still challenging. I still choose to drive down old roads in my mind that no longer serve me.

I still get stuck making hard decisions and being fearful that I've messed it all up. My old programs, old beliefs, and old stories still have a place in my mind, and they still take over sometimes. I used to call these challenging times, "Ditch Moments." These were moments where my fear was overriding my faith, where I felt like I was stuck in a state of darkness, depression, and uncertainty.

After I had popped out of one of my most challenging ditch moments, I started to recognize all the lessons, the growth, and the leveling up I had done because of this moment. I started to feel grateful for this moment in time. I started to see the domino effect of how it had ultimately led to bigger, brighter realizations and how it made me into a better and more evolved coach and teacher.

I started to finally recognize that we live in a universe that abides by the law of duality and that light/dark, love/fear, happiness/sadness are two sides of the same coin, and you cannot fully experience one without the other.

I began to embrace the ditch moment, and then I wrote a new belief and a new story about how ditch moments are actually "cocoon moments," moments that feel dark and scary but are really preparing you for a leveling up and a transformation that literally creates a new version of you. And, poof, just like magic, "ditch moments" died, and "cocoon moments" were born, and I was able to see life's challenges through a whole different lens that I could share with my clients as well.

Everyone in my world started having "cocoon moments" and proudly sharing them with me. Their perspective changed and their vibration upleveled too. My shift in perspective and my choosing to see life in a positive way was having a ripple effect that was impacting people all around me. It was a beautiful revelation and experience and one that I remind myself of often, so I can keep the momentum moving in the right direction.

Choosing the new road, the one where you may not know all the turns and you may not know exactly what the destination looks and sounds and feels like is the way towards happiness, fulfillment, growth, and evolving to the next level where your faith is stronger than your fear and your life is brighter than you expected.

Exercise:

Consider an old thought pattern, story, or belief. What are the thoughts that lead to the beliefs that create the story you're telling over and over? Write the whole story here. What are the thoughts you think and say repeatedly? What is the story behind it? How did it come to be this way? How do you know it's so true? What benefit do you get out of telling the story over and over? Then, rewrite it.

Rewrite an entirely different story. Rewrite the opposite thoughts and turn the beliefs over. What would it sound like if you came from a place of faith instead of fear when you tell this story? What are the lessons you've learned? How have you positively changed because of this story?

Start to see the blessing instead of the burden in it. Rewrite it from that perspective. When you're all done, see if you can shift to a new road on this story. What does the new road look and sound and feel like? Live in that. Embrace that. See what else shifts in your life as a result. Look for the ripple effect.

Sending you good juju. You got this.

NATALIE SUSI

About Natalie Susi: Natalie has more than fourteen years of experience as a teacher, speaker, entrepreneur, and mentor. Currently, she's a five-year UCSD professor focusing on communications and the Pursuit of Happiness. As an entrepreneur, she founded and grew Bare Organic Mixers beverage company for eight years, resulting in an acquisition in 2014.

After selling the company, Natalie combined her educational background as a teacher and her experience as an entrepreneur to provide personal development coaching and consulting to individuals, businesses, and creative entrepreneurs. She developed a program called Conscious Conversations and utilizes a step-by-step process called The Alignment Method to support leaders in cultivating conscious teams and businesses through a process of self-reflection, self-discover, and self-ascension that ultimately increases profits, productivity, and the growth of the individuals, personally and professionally.

Author's Website: *www.NatalieSusi.com*

Book Series Website: *www.The13StepsToRiches.com*

Nita Patel

BROADCASTING SYNCHRONICITIES TO BECOMING RICH

The subconscious mind, auto-suggestion, and the creative imagination are key components of the brain when it comes to growing rich, and it all begins with desire. Napoleon Hill brings all the components together in this chapter as he further explains to his audience how various aspects of our brain come into play with respect to success in life. After all, the title of his book was *Think and Grow Rich.* It wasn't work hard and grow rich, be smart and grow rich, or even get an education and grow rich.

As we've seen in the world around us today, there are many wealthy people who are not educated in the traditional sense. There are many rich people who probably would not score high on an IQ test. And so many people work so hard and still are at the poverty line. All these examples demonstrate Napoleon Hill's teachings on the *"Think"* part of the title. Let's take a deeper dive into how we can use our brain to achieve success or grow rich in essence.

For starters, what does rich mean to you? Defining what rich means to you personally determines your success. There are numerous studies which show that defining a goal and writing it down automatically increases your chances of achieving them. What does being rich mean to you? Does it mean not being in debt? Does it mean having your necessities met with ease? Does it mean you can buy anything you want or help others without thinking twice?

Or does it mean you're not stuck in a job you hate and being able to explore your passion and do something where your talents and skills are valued? Are you the person who's set an arbitrary number to what rich mean? I used to be that person who decided a random number that made me feel emotionally safe.

I once told my boss that I needed a three thousand-dollar raise. He asked me why. And instead of responding with what I was going to do with the money, I responded with something random like well I decided that when I turn x age, I would be making x amount. He laughed at me and continued questioning me.

I didn't have the awareness at the time to clearly communicate an unfiltered response. I was responding with what I thought would be general enough so that he would just agree to it. He eventually met me halfway, but had I been specific to convey my value or self-worth, I would've received the amount I asked for. He told me not to set arbitrary goals in life, which was not the case at all, but I was not brave enough to ask for what I wanted. I didn't know how to value myself with confidence at the time, which bring me to step number two: Confidence Sells.

Napoleon Hill talks about how your brain is a broadcasting station. The collective thoughts you suggest to yourself (also known as Autosuggestion) is the frequency you're broadcasting. When someone else has their receiver tuned to the same frequency synchronicities happen. This is how people come into your orbit. When you exude confidence and demand your worth, the fake people shy away and fall out of your orbit because they are on a different frequency.

To achieve your goals and become rich, you must act with confidence. You must have faith (as we discussed in the Faith chapter) that what you are asking for will be given to you. And when you broadcast that signal, the synchronicities give you the people you need to support you on your journey to becoming rich.

Recent discoveries have proven that elevated feelings are key to manifesting positive outcomes. Visualization (or Creative Imagination) is a traditional method to faking your brain into believing you've achieved a goal. Athletes have been using this method for decades.

They visualize winning a race over and over again, which convinces their brain that the body knows what to do to win. Seeing it happen in their mind over and over gives the brain the confidence it needs to know it's not only possible but that it's a sure thing. Once this belief has been embedded in the subconscious mind, it sends the appropriate signals to the body of such performance, and the body follows the orders.

Let's walk through a simple example. How many times have you gone to the gym with the intention of working out, but your mind is telling you (or you are telling your mind) you're so tired, you didn't sleep enough last night, you don't have energy, it's going to be a quick workout, you're really hungry; whatever the thousands of excuses are that we find when we don't really want to do something.

Because of this autosuggestion, you've already convinced yourself that it's okay not to put your best effort in before you even get to the gym. When you get there, your body is prepared to follow all the orders from that autosuggestion. You end up performing very similar to your expectation.

This is the power of the brain. I've shared this in a previous chapter, but it's pertinent to share again. Your body is like a dumb terminal; it does whatever your brain tells it to do.

This example demonstrates how we behave the way we do, but also how an Olympian wins a race. And if you're wondering why you are in the position you are in, take a moment to introspect on how you use your brain and what things you can change to achieve your goals.

And with all that said, I'd like to give you a life hack. Yes, you still have to do the work to understand where you're at and what you really want. But once you figure that out, there's a simpler way to shift the frequencies you emit. You might think of it as a cheat code, but it's completely natural. There are sound frequencies you can use to program your brain and body to be in elevated states.

Additionally, there are devices that emit electromagnetic energies, which expedite raising your frequency even faster. Many of these devices use the Tesla coil to conduct energy. These are science-based technologies and machines that can be used to hack the mind into higher frequencies.

A combination of these methods can be applied into convincing your brain what you deserve. You deserve your very best. It doesn't have the be the same as what anyone else defines as the best. If it's good enough for you, you're already rich!

NITA PATEL

About Nita Patel: Nita is a bestselling author, speaker, and artist who believes in modern etiquette as a path to becoming our best selves. Through her professional years, Ms. Patel has twenty-five years of demonstrated technology leadership experience in various industries, specifically with a concentrated focus on health care, for fourteen of those twenty-plus years. She's shown her art across the world, including the Louvre in Paris.

She's a Bestselling Author and performance coach, pursuing her master's in industrial organizational (I-O) psychology at Harvard. Her investment in psychology theory and practice is what led her to a deep interest in helping others. She has become deeply and passionately devoted to nurturing others and in building their confidence and brand through speaking and consultative practices.

Author's Website: *www.Nita-Patel.com*

Book Series Website: *www.The13StepsToRiches.com*

Phillip D. McClure

THE ULTIMATE GATEWAY TO RICHES

As I reflect upon the journey that has brought me here, my mind wanders to our most complex organ, the brain. Our most mysterious organ serves as the twelfth step on our path towards riches—our master control center, seat of consciousness, and source of creativity.

While exploring its mysteries, I am reminded of John Assaraf's significant influence in shaping my understanding of this remarkable organ through groundbreaking works like *Innercise* and *Having It All*, which have shed light onto many peoples' journeys toward riches, including mine. Thanks, John Assaraf!

Brainpower is not limited to thoughts; it's where our deepest beliefs, fears, and aspirations take root. My quest to understand my brain's importance in creating riches began earnestly during a dark and early morning drive to work. Witnessing a restored pickup truck careen off the road and explode into flames before my eyes was an eye-opener—it highlighted my brain's extraordinary capacity for adaptability in times of extreme stress.

Military training took over, and without conscious thought, I found myself pulling an injured driver out of the wreckage. This act of subconscious bravery, triggered by my brain's fight-or-flight response, ultimately saved their life on that fateful day and taught me firsthand about the power of the subconscious mind—something John Assaraf emphasizes strongly in his teachings.

My grandfather's story, Corporal Taylor's, illustrates my brain's capacity for working under extreme conditions by showing its quiet focus while acquiring specialized knowledge. His mission behind enemy lines during one of history's darkest chapters proved my brain's capacity for problem-solving and innovation under pressure with his expertise in battlefield mechanics, team spirit, and courage turning the tide of an otherwise catastrophic situation—a fantastic testament of how knowledge combined with expertise can help overcome seemingly insurmountable barriers and achieve success.

This tale passed down through generations is a powerful testimony that shows just how powerfully knowledge combined with skills can overcome seemingly insurmountable obstacles!

Since childhood, imagination has been my trusted companion. My imagination has always driven my aspirations and goals, from racing go-karts to dreaming up grand achievements. John Assaraf masterfully used imagination as the centerpiece of goal achievement through thought power; vivid scenes we create in our mind's eye are not mere daydreams but blueprints of our future realities. My journey from imaginary racetracks in my youth to actualizing my goals is a testament to this fantastic tool: our brain's creative ability!

Brain power in our pursuit of riches goes beyond simply amassing wealth; instead, its role involves giving life meaning, passion, and fulfillment. Through my stories—from fiery rescues to battlefield victories and flights of imagination—I aim to demonstrate different aspects of brain capabilities; each narrative emphasizes the importance of nurturing our minds by continuously learning, challenging perceptions, and encouraging creative prowess.

In this chapter, I aim to assemble these threads into a coherent arras that highlights the brain's critical role in our pursuit of riches. Drawing from my personal experiences and wisdom imparted by John Assaraf, I will explore how our subconscious minds, specialized knowledge, and imagination play a critical role in unlocking our immense potential as individuals. Remember that the brain is more than an organ; it's the gateway to an abundant and prosperous lifestyle!

As I build on the foundation established in earlier sections, I want to explore in greater depth some personal anecdotes that have informed my understanding of the brain's immense capabilities. These stories from my own life and those before mine provide vivid illustrations of how the brain orchestrates our journey towards riches—not just materially but in terms of experiences and fulfillment.

One story that stands out in my memory involves life-saving intuition. It occurred during an incident involving an overturned, flaming truck—when every second counted, and the margin for error was nonexistent. Within the chaos and inferno lay an instantaneous decision with life-or-death implications that I needed to make quickly based on instinctual knowledge and acquired expertise.

My brain's ability to process complex situations quickly guided my actions in making this crucial choice. This was no ordinary physical bravery but rather an inspiring display of mental fortitude, proving my brain could function under tremendous stress to filter out noise and focus solely on saving a life. John Assaraf's teachings on the subconscious mind seemed to come alive right before my eyes as I navigated through flames and wreckage.

Another profound demonstration of the brain's role in creating wealth comes from my grandfather, Corporal Taylor's battlefield account. His mission behind enemy lines, fraught with danger and uncertainty, highlighted the necessity of specialized knowledge and an individual's capacity for innovation in times of difficulty. Problem-solving skills were instrumental in turning an urgent situation into a compelling rescue mission.

Generation after generation has been reminded of this tale, which illustrates our brain's limitless capabilities when presented with challenges, reinforcing our belief that with adequate knowledge and a mindset for problem-solving, we can overcome virtually all obstacles we encounter.

These personal narratives infused with neuroscience wisdom and John Assaraf's mentorship demonstrate the brain's vital role in navigating a journey to riches. We can tap our true potential only by understanding and harnessing its powers—its subconscious instincts, knowledge, and limitless imagination. As we explore its capabilities, let us remain ever mindful that we may be setting off a chain reaction toward living lives full of purpose, passion, and prosperity.

One of the most exciting parts of contributing to this book series has been having the chance and privilege of co-authoring with John Assaraf, whose genius and mentorship have profoundly shaped my journey. John's deep understanding of how the brain operates and his remarkable talent for translating complex neuroscience into actionable strategies have been transformative for me.

His books and teachings have enhanced my knowledge of how the mind works and provided strength through personal and professional challenges. My longstanding respect and admiration for John have given this project enormous personal significance.

Collaboration goes beyond mere authorship; it represents a meeting of minds with shared passions and an eagerness to tap into humanity's undiscovered riches. This experience was essential to honoring John Assaraf's lasting impression on my life and paying my gratitude. It was a testament to his mentorship, leaving an indelible mark on my journey of understanding and harnessing brainpower.

PHILLIP D. MCCLURE

About Phillip D. McClure: Phillip is married to the love of his life, Maaike McClure, and is a very proud father of two exciting kids. He was raised in the great state of Montana before moving to Utah.

Phil lives life to the fullest. His accomplishments consist of completing a full Ironman, and deploying four times with the Army, earning multiple decorations along the way—including two Utah crosses! This makes him the only soldier in history to receive that medal twice.

Currently, Phil is the Owner of NorthStar Coins, Events by NorthStar, the co-owner of P.B. Fast Cars, and recruits pilots for the Army Aviation program. It was during his last deployment that he accidentally created his first Mastermind and it has forever changed his life as well as the others involved. He mentors and coaches in self-improvement and physical fitness.

Phil is an exotic car enthusiast who spends as much time behind the wheel as possible, whether it is carving through canyons, ripping around the racetrack, or coaching others to see their potential. Competitive driving is the best therapy in the world.

Live life to the fullest and have fun while doing it. You don't get a rewind in life so take mistakes as the lessons they are and improve, but don't make the same mistakes twice.

Live in flow, not with the flow.

Author's Website: *www.NorthStarCoins.com*

Book Series Website: *www.The13StepsToRiches.com*

Robyn Scott

MY FAVORITE NUMBER 13

Chapter 13 in *Think and Grow Rich* speaks about the brain almost from a spiritual point of view. It sees the brain as a broadcasting system and receiving station for vibrations of thought. In short, this chapter explains that it is very important you keep yourself motivated and in the right mood, so your brain works at full capacity. This will allow you to think more clearly and will help you receive inspiration easily.

Over the past year, I have had many adventures with MY brain! It is an extreme eye-opener, and I would love to share my experience with my journey with my brain. I know I am not the only out there dealing with my brain journey as well!

Last year, I slept about three hours a night. I felt great! My energy level was through the roof, and I was kind of all over the place as far as energy goes, except it was high, fun energy! I felt like I was in a whole new vibration—or so I thought. I am completely aware that my brain is not like anyone else's (I might have forgotten—with such little sleep, I forgot A LOT). I had people depending on me! I had amazing projects in my sight, and, at the end of the day, I spent three days in the hospital, and the diagnosis was bipolar depression. (I wish I could add the shock eye emoji here.)

I was raised by a bipolar mom. In 2016, I found my birth mother…guess what? She is bipolar, too. I had resigned to the fact that I was also suffering from bipolar depression. At forty-nine years old, I felt exponentially terrified and a little comforted that I had done this for so long! I can handle this—with grace. I have so far!

I lost all my positions in the businesses I was a part of; I was not reliable any longer. My family was extremely frustrated with my flightiness and absentmindedness and, truly, not being able to focus on any task. I felt like I was being betrayed by my own brain. After seeing doctors and getting on new meds, we realized I did not have a bipolar prognosis. I was chemically resistant.

My heart was a little relieved until I started feeling what that looked like. I looked back over the many years of my life and noticed a pattern. Every other year or so, I have a major health crisis. I now believe that I created those scenarios with my brain, and the vibrations I created brought this right back to me. Migraines, colon infection, and septic shock, not even realizing I even had a kidney infection. I got serotonin syndrome from all the meds my doctor was prescribing. I only went into the hospital, with no sleep for months, to stop a nosebleed I had for ten hours. I was not listening to me at all! I do know that our brains are WAY more powerful than we can understand.

The important point here is not to stick to the exact description Napoleon Hill does in chapter 13 of *The Brain*, described as a broadcasting station of thought. Instead, we have to look at what he meant, which is certainly still true today: brainstorming might excite your brain and increase its creativity.

We all know that being motivated and in the right mood makes us more sensitive to the environment, increases our mental faculties, and improves our social skills when we interact with others.

If you want to look at this fact the way Napoleon Hill did, there is no problem about it. If you want to look at this with a more contemporary approach, it is also fine. The important point here is you feel comfortable as long as you keep on stimulating your brain in order to increase its performance (memory, social skills, creativity, etc.).

Think and Grow Rich Chapter 13 might seem confusing. At this point, Napoleon Hill turns a little bit mystic, and some clarifications are needed. It is important to keep in mind the book was written in 1937, and at that time, science was not as developed as today. At that time, some pseudo-sciences like phrenology were in vogue, and occult sciences were certainly widespread across the United States (*Think and Grow Rich Summary Online*).

"We are now entering the most marvelous of all ages. An age which will teach us something of the intangible forces of the world about us. Perhaps we shall learn, as we pass through this age, that the "other self" is more powerful than the physical self we see when we look into a mirror.

Sometimes, men speak lightly of the intangibles—the things that they cannot perceive through any of their five senses, and when we hear them, it should remind us that all of us are controlled by forces that are unseen and intangible.

The whole of mankind does not have the power to cope with or control the intangible force wrapped up in the rolling waves of the oceans. Man does not have the capacity to understand the intangible force of gravity, which keeps this little earth suspended in mid-air and keeps man from falling from it, much less the power to control that force. Man is entirely subservient to the intangible force which comes with a thunderstorm, and he is just as helpless in the presence of the intangible force of electricity —nay, he does not even know what electricity is, where it comes from, or what is its purpose!

Nor is this by any means the end of man's ignorance in connection with things unseen and intangible. He does not understand the intangible force (and intelligence) wrapped up in the soil of the earth--the force that provides him with every morsel of food he eats, every article of clothing he wears, and every dollar he carries in his pockets (Sacred Texts)."

Napoleon really spoke to me in this chapter. It is fascinating to think of all the power we have. I know we create our own worlds. I also believed I needed to be in an altered state to pull out my creativity, my innovations, and my contributions to any creative project. I was insecure and intimidated. Maybe I was afraid to show up by just being me? Do I know who that is? Am I enough?

I was fearful and secretive about how my brain works. I kept quiet in meetings, fearing I'd embarrass myself or others I was working with. And I did. It was after I created a huge mess within myself that I am still picking up pieces, mending relationships, and moving forward with my brain! That is the best part of our brains! This is where I want to introduce you to the "Unicorn Factor!"

The Unicorn Factor. I have been called a unicorn many, many times. I love it! I freaking am a unicorn, AND SO ARE YOU! Even with my crazy brain, I have come to terms of being different, weird, hyper, too much! It is one of my powers. I am unapologetic. I don't really notice I may need to apologize, so it's a new skill for me. The world needs YOU to tell your story, to speak YOUR truth, to engage! No one on this planet, deceased or not born yet, has their "absotively and positutely" OWN PERCEPTION! There is no maybe or not might be, as each of us have perfectly unicornish experiences!

Twins with the same DNA, same physical features, same upbringing, same mother, father, sister, brother, etc. Not even they have the same perspective! That's the fun part of life! If you can look at that, it brings things into a different point of view! How incredibly boring would our world be with us being the same! Including our failures, all our loves, all our heartbreak, our traumatic experiences, along with our championships and glories! Each experience we have had in this lifetime needs to be shared! Our stories are the survival guide for those who come after us! Tell your story!

When healing your brain, stay close to YOU! Be motivated for certain, if that means just getting out of bed! YOU DID IT! (Been there!)

I started a treatment that actually mapped out where my brain was not activated and REMAPPED IT! Transcranial magnetic stimulation (TMS) is a safe, effective treatment for depression, OCD, PTSD, anxiety, and other mental illnesses. TMS treatment (or TMS therapy) uses magnetic pulses, similar to an MRI, to stimulate brain function and cause the brain to develop new neural pathways. These new pathways give the brain the ability to overcome the negative effects of major depression, OCD, anxiety, PTSD, and other illnesses. Patients who undergo TMS treatment report a 75% success rate in achieving significant alleviation of symptoms and a 51% success rate in achieving remission of symptoms—an astounding success rate!

Talk to your provider! Surround yourself with like-minded people! BE YOU! Stimulate that noggin! We can stay in our brains a little too much sometimes. Getting your mind to quiet and be still is a challenge for me, and I know that is where my true power lies! GO FORTH, YOU UNICORN!

Bibliography

Think and Grow Rich Summary Online, *ThinkAndGrowRichSummary.online/summary/chapter-13/*

Sacred Texts, *Sacred-Texts.com/nth/tgr/tgr18.htm*

ROBYN SCOTT

About Robyn Scott: Robyn manages the prospecting program for Divinely Driven Results. Robyn is a Habit Finder Coach and has worked closely with the president, Paul Blanchard, at the Og Mandino Group. She is also a certified Master Your Emotions Coach through Inscape World. Robyn is commonly known in professional communities as the Queen of Connection and Princess of Play. She has been working hard for the past nine years to hone her skills as a mentor and coach. Scott strives to teach people to annihilate judgments, embrace their own stories, and empower themselves to rediscover who they truly are. Scott is an international speaker who teaches you how to present yourself on stage.

Her first book, *Bringing People Together: Rediscovering the Lost Art of Face-to-Face Connecting, Collaborating, and Creating,* was released in August 2019 and was a bestseller in seven categories.

Author's Website: *www.RobynKayeScott.com*

Book Series Website: *www.The13StepsToRiches.com*

Dr. Shannon Whittington

MORE BRAIN HACKS

The brain is fascinating, mysterious, and a marvelous instrument. Weighing only three pounds, it is the powerhouse of memory, knowledge, cognition, and joy. Impressively, a tiny speck of brain tissue holds up to 100,000 neurons, which can travel up to 268 miles per hour!

It is also the source of our deepest selves. What happens in our brain controls not only our thoughts but also our destinies. Despite its inherent mystery, we can perform hacks to make our brains work in our favor and help move us forward toward achieving long-term success. Let me share with you some of my hacks that have worked wonders for me.

Move that Body

It can't be overstated enough how beneficial exercise is for our brain and our body. According to the Center for Disease Control (CDC), most adults benefit from engaging in 150 minutes of exercise per week, which can be broken down into 30 minutes a day, five days a week (*CDC.gov*). By taking a short amount of time each day to move our bodies, we're better situated to retain information, multitask, and problem-solving, not to mention stave off depression, anxiety, and even dementia.

While doing simple workouts aid your brain, try to take at least one day per week to perform high-intensity interval training (HIIT), a form of exercise consisting of short periods of intense movement alternated with less intense periods of recovery. HIIT workouts can help promote growth of new brain cells and neuronal circuits, and it's especially helpful to utilize sports-centric movements by setting spatial targets around you, aiding in your cognition. You can do these workouts pretty much anywhere, and there are tons of YouTube videos dedicated to HIIT workouts that you can take advantage of.

Meditate

Meditation is one of the most useful ways to benefit our brain. For many of us, meditation can seem virtually impossible. But take heart, engaging in meditation doesn't mean you have to be perfect at it. In fact, just the act alone of *trying* to silence our thoughts and focus on our breath can do us a world of good. According to Synchronicity.org, meditation allows the brain to process information faster, improve focus, attention, cognition, and mood, and synchronize our right and left hemispheres (*Synchronicity.org*). For me, when I meditate regularly, I notice that I am way more calm and I make decisions quicker and a lot easier.

While the thought of sitting down and focusing solely on our breathing can be a challenge for some of us, it's a challenge worth exploring. You can seek out guided meditation sessions through apps like Calm or Headspace, or YouTube University. Also, you can simply take a few minutes each day to sit and breathe, allowing your thoughts to come and go and returning to the balance of your breath. There is magic in that practice alone.

Think Positive

There is no need to mention how difficult life can be. We all have a chapter we can write. From work stress to financial worries and beyond, it can be difficult to look on the bright side of things. Yet, when we take the time to intentionally think positively, our mood improves, and our brain benefits. According to Meteor Education, thinking positively "increases mental productivity, intensifies [our] ability to pay attention… improves [our] ability to think and analyze incoming data, [and] improves [our] ability to solve problems quicker and enhance creativity" (*MeteorEducation.com*).

Something that helps me navigate my daily stressors is thinking about the people in my life that I love the most: family, friends, trusted mentors, etc. I focus on the things that I'm grateful for, and I look towards the future about the things I desire, whether they be new and continued relationships, exciting personal and business ventures, or material things that would be nice to have. Intentionally thinking positively tricks my brain into doing so out of habit, leading me to better places and achieved goals.

Set Mini-Goals

Goal-setting is like a superfood for our brains. Inc. Magazine mentions that "goal-setting literally alters the structure of our brains so that we perceive and behave in ways that will cause us to achieve said goals." While setting longer-term goals is great, our brains also benefit from setting shorter-term goals as well. This is because our brain enjoys instant gratification, and achieving mini goals provides us with dopamine boosts.

For example, let's say you're working on a large-scale project, and you're feeling overwhelmed as if it's never going to be accomplished. Take a moment to ask yourself, "How can I break this goal down into smaller, more manageable 'mini-goals'?" When you write out a list of each mini-goal, your brain instantly sees each one as something that can be more easily accomplished, leading you to achieve your overall big goal in the long run.

I did this by getting my doctorate, and believe me, it worked. I didn't look at how long it would take or the twelve classes I had to complete. I looked at each class as a mini class and once I completed that class, I simply moved to the next one. Until one day, low and behold, I realized I had nearly crossed the finish line! This made the task of acquiring something difficult much easier because I broke it down into tiny steps. This did wonders for my psyche.

Making mini goals also helps our brain to set goals unrelated to work projects, such as vacuuming the floor, cleaning the kitchen, or finishing a load of laundry. When our brain recognizes the task as complete, it gives our brain a reward and amps us up to take on the next work-related task.

Declutter

Do you work in an environment that's on the messy side? Trust me, I've been there. If so, you're not doing yourself or your brain any favors; you're actually making your day a lot harder than it needs to be. Our brain not only gets visually overwhelmed with unnecessary clutter, but it also sees our work environments as reflections of ourselves, thereby lowering our self-esteem. This is why it's important to make sure that you're working in an environment that is as tidy as possible.

One of my colleagues was always behind on everything at work, and her desk looked like a hurricane had hit it and came back a second time. One day, I came in to work early, and together, we did a deep decluttering of her desk. Later that day, she told me how she felt calmer and was able to accomplish more in a day than she had in a week, simply because her desk was decluttered!

If you're feeling overwhelmed with the amount of clutter in your workspace, take my earlier advice and set mini-goals for yourself. Work on one area of your desk at a time and then organize your computer desktop as well. Little acts like these can go a long way in making you feel a lot less overwhelmed and much more productive. I did this in my mom's living room just last week. Each day, I did only one corner at a time. After four days, the living room looked spotless, and Mom was loving me for it!

Read

It should come as no surprise that reading books stimulates our brain. According to Inc. Magazine, "reading...[rewires] how our brain works...strengthens our ability to imagine alternative paths, remember details, picture detailed scenes, and think through complex problems. In short, reading makes us more knowledgeable and functionally smarter." Reading boosts our empathy by putting us in unique situations by providing us with lived experiences unlike our own, giving us access to perspectives we may have not ever known.

Our busy schedules may make it seem like we simply don't have time to devour books the way many of us did when we were in school and college. The good news? You don't have to read a ton each day to get the mental and emotional benefits.

By simply setting aside half an hour to an hour each day to read, whether it's a romance novel or a history book, or something else entirely, you're providing your brain with an assortment of nutritive and feel-good chemicals that can better help you as you work to achieve your goals. As for me, I've become a fan of audible and I now devour books on my long walks with my dog. This has been a real game changer for me.

All of these tricks can go a long way in boosting your brain and helping you achieve your goals. Above all, remember to take time to celebrate each mini-goal you achieve and be patient with yourself. Rewiring our brains is not an overnight task; it takes practice and dedication, but I promise you it's worth it in the long haul. Because we all know the old saying: a mind is a terrible thing to waste.

References

www.cdc.gov/nccdphp/dnpao/features/physical-activity-brain-health/index.html

www.synchronicity.org/blogs/blog/free-infographic-effects-of-meditation-on-the-brain

www.meteoreducation.com/how-does-thinking-positive-thoughts-affect-neuroplasticity

SHANNON WHITTINGTON

About Dr. Shannon Whittington: Shannon (she/her) is a speaker, author, consultant, and clinical nurse educator. Her area of expertise is LGBTQ+ inclusion in the workplace. Whittington has a passion for transgender health where she educates clinicians in how to care for transgender individuals after undergoing gender-affirming surgeries.

Whittington was honored to receive the Quality and Innovation Award from the Home Care Association of New York for her work with the transgender population. She was recently awarded the Notable LGBTQ+ Leaders & Executives award by Crain's New York Business, Daisy Award for Outstanding Nurses, as well as the International Association of Professionals Nurse of the Year award. Whittington is a city and state lobbyist for transgender equality.

To date, Whittington has presented virtually and in person at various organizations and conferences across the nation, delivering extremely well-received presentations. Her forthcoming books include *LGBTQ+: ABC's For Grownups* and *Kindergarten for Leaders: 9 Essential Tips For Grownup Success.*

Author's Website: *www.linkedin.com/in/ShannonWhittington*

Book Series Website: *www.The13StepsToRiches.com*

Soraiya Vasanji

BLIND SPOTS

Fascinated and Obsessed. I was thoroughly fascinated and obsessed with Neuroscience and Biopsychology in my undergraduate studies. Professor Klaus Miczek, the Moses Hunt Professor of Psychology, Psychiatry, Pharmacology, and Neuroscience, and who serves as one of the directors of the Neuroscience Research Center at Tufts University, was my professor for many of these classes.

I remember how astounded I was when I first learned of the relationship between the brain, the eye, and how vision works. Did you know that we see upside down? Well, technically, the images received on our retina, at the back of the eye, are inverted and the brain makes them right side up. How cool, right? Imagine if we had to try and coordinate our arms and legs in an upside-down world. How crazy would that be? Professor Miczek taught us the structure of the eye and the fundamentals of brain behavior, which ended up being what I majored in at Tufts.

The National Eye Institute shares this diagram which I can still picture and draw 2 decades later with my eyes closed.

Their simplified explanation of sight includes, "When light hits the **retina** (a light-sensitive layer of tissue at the back of the eye), special cells called photoreceptors turn the light into electrical signals. These electrical signals travel from the retina through the **optic nerve** to the brain. Then the brain turns the signals into the images you see."

239

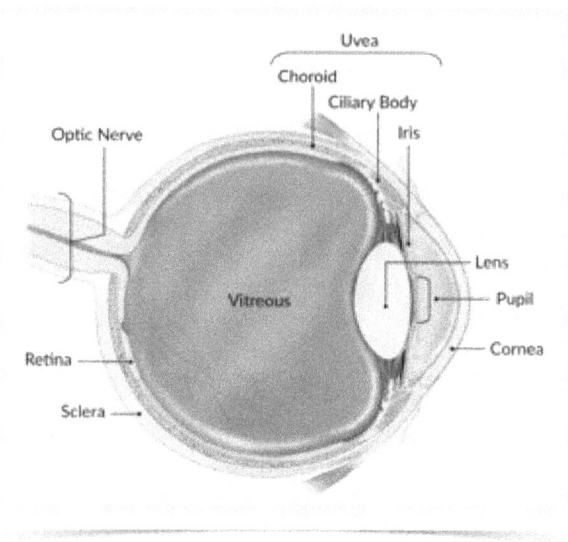

Now you might be wondering why I am sharing so much about the eye and vision, but it actually helps to understand how the brain works. I also love to geek out on the brain and the eye because so much of our life is based on *what we see and how we "see" things in our life*. Therefore, I think it is vastly fundamental to understand *how we see* to realize that so much of our inner world and outer world is created by our brain and what it shows or lights up in front of us.

The Blind Spot Test

Even with all we *can see,* there is a portion of the eye where the optic nerves converge to leave the eye known as the optic disc. Light rays are not detected in this area so there is a break in the visuals coming into the eye, which is referred to as the blind spot. You can do a quick test of this on the next page. There be an X and an O. Cover your right eye and have your left eye focus on the X. Move the page away from your eye. Try varying the distance by putting the book a few feet away and staring at the X. Keep looking at the X and now step closer or away from the page.

At some point, the circle in your peripheral vision will become invisible and your brain will fill in the area with whatever cues it can. In this case, filling the space with the white page. A quick Google search will show you more Blind Spot tests that are fun to do at home. While research is still ongoing about the brain and how it interprets information in the optic disc, it has always made me curious about blind spots—both physical and mental.

Give it a try. See *The Blind Spot Test* on the next page.

O   X

What is your blind spot?

What are you not attuned to?

What are you not seeing in your life?

What are you ignoring or pretending not to see or not to know?

When someone is in the space of compassionate self-curiosity and ready to create the changes they wish to make in their life, another line of questioning I like to ask is around what bothers them. What repetitive triggers/traits consistently show up in their life? How does this show up in other areas of their life, and what would their life look like if the personality annoyance didn't show up as often? Knowing they are turning a blind eye to the behavior or thought that they wish wouldn't show up, what are they prepared to create to let this go?

Personally, when I took the time to look at my blind spots, I found a recurrent one that I was ready to shift. I found I would create tardiness or lateness and easily get annoyed at myself for doing this and doing this over and over again. No amount of leaving early or alarms would shift this because there was something I was not seeing. When I knew I was going to be late, I would get fired up and annoyed and distract myself from something else. Yet, I seemed to always cut it close and think that I had more time than I actually did. I would be late by a few minutes to physiotherapy appointments or late to a play date.

It would also show up when I would think I had more time than I actually did. For example, in the last hour of preparation before guests would be coming over to our house for game night, I would still have a mega to do list going including: setting the table, chopping the salad, baking the appetizer, arranging the charcuterie board with the Tiktok salami flower and, of course, style my hair. *(Yes, I always had to drop a couple of those things and hubby had to rescue me—at least he makes an awesome cheese board in a flash now!)*

What was my blind spot, though? What was I not seeing or ready to see? Turns out, after a lot of inner inquiry, my unique, personal answer was that I thought I had to do so much and have a productive day in order to feel like I was worthy. Specific to the dinner party, I believed that I had to do all those things to impress my guests for them to think I was somehow worthy. It boiled down to: **I needed to DO a lot in order to FEEL enough.**

Sometimes our habits or actions, like me thinking I have more time than I do or that I can fit more things into little periods of time, have a deeper-rooted thought in our values or belief system. Trying to solve this problem by cramming less in or leaving more space to get somewhere didn't work long term. It was the consistent actions of re-learning that I was good enough as I was and that I didn't need to do more to have a "productive day." I wasn't being measured by this. Once I let that go, I could play with time in a different way and make space for quality moments and not be late to appointments!

What blind spots are getting in the way of living your best life?

What is your brain telling you or making up for you so you can continue to avoid the changes you desperately want to have the life you dream of?

Our Prefrontal Cortex & Neural Pathways that Keep Us Safe

Our brain and the thoughts that circulate want to keep us safe. One part of our brain called the prefrontal cortex at the top of our head is believed to largely be responsible for our fear responses. Our fear responses include Fight, Flight, Freeze, Flop or Friend. As human beings, it was more important to be aware of the dangers and scan for threats than to focus on other information, particularly positive things. Hence, stress and anxiety are prevalent feelings we carry around at some degree constantly.

Our neural pathways, the connections formed in one part of the brain that send messages to another part of the brain, light up every time we have that thought and are the basis of our habits. Creating new neural pathways help to shift our behaviors. It is why we love routines and knowing what comes next. Think of a toddler and the routines we set up, such as an evening routine that might include eating, bathing, brushing, reading, and sleep time. We follow these patterns and they become easier and signal our body for what comes next.

Our brain can become so used to thinking or acting a certain way that we don't even realize that we have just trained ourselves to think or do something in a certain way. What if we learned or believed things that are not real but we are so used to seeing things a certain way that we are unwilling to be open minded that it could mean something else?

As humans, we judge and interpret other people's actions or words as ammunition against us, when in actuality the majority of the time other people's thoughts and actions have nothing to do with us. We just make it mean something about us. What if we can be open minded and challenge our current neural pathways that are trying to keep the status quo and keep us safe?

What would actually be helpful in these situations is to catch our thoughts and re-evaluate them based on maximizing future pleasure and minimizing past pain. Challenge your own thinking—you are allowed! I give you permission!

Emotional Response

The parts of the brain most related to emotional response and memory would be the amygdala and the hippocampus. What I didn't realize until I started to experiment with essential oils, potent chemical compounds of plants, is that inhaling these aromatic chemical components stimulate these areas of the brain where our emotional and episodic memory and feelings reside. It's like when you smell freshly baked cookies and are reminded of being back in your grandmother's kitchen and feeling safe and cared for. Who doesn't want a warm chocolate chip cookie?

When you come into contact with a particular smell, and in this case these chemical compounds found in nature, they can support eliciting specific feelings. I first began gifting essential oils to my clients as thank yous because I personally enjoyed using them. Then I started to see patterns in how my fertility clients were processing grief and moving through emotions better, and I started to see entrepreneurs letting go of past mistakes a little easier and breathing deeper and plunging forward with greater ease.

I want to be clear that essential oils are not curing anything. However, they have a place in supporting our thoughts and emotions especially when we are wanting to process or shift emotions that we get stuck in. It's like that hit of energetic awakeness when you cut into a citrus fruit. It's not huge, but your mood shifts slightly, regardless.

I enjoy following the real science behind quality essential oils and not the majority of diluted and adulterated stuff you find at big box retailers or online platforms. Make sure you are asking about potency and purity if you are looking to buy some. Who knows? You might be a smell away from uncovering your blind spot!

SORAIYA VASANJI

About Soraiya Vasanji: Soraiya is a Certified Professional Coach (CPC), Energy Leadership Index Master Practitioner (ELI-MP), and has a Master's in Business Administration (MBA) from Kellogg University. She inspires women to be present, not perfect, ditch what doesn't serve them, and create their best messy life now.

She loves sharing her wisdom on mindset, the power of language, self-love, self-worth, and leadership principles. She is the founder of the Mommy Mindset Summit series, and the Mom Mindset Reset Method coaching program. She empowers moms to move from tired, frustrated and depleted in their life to a creating the calm, happy and emotional even life for them and their families - no longer swinging from "energizer bunny mom" to dead on the couch!

Soraiya is married to her soulmate, has a young daughter, and lives in Toronto, Canada. She is a foodie, a jetsetter, a doTERRA essential oil enthusiast and she loves collecting unique crafting and stationery products!

Author's Website: *www.SoraiyaVasanji.com*

Book Series Website: *www.The13StepsToRiches.com*

Stacey Ross Cohen

YOUR BRAIN IS A POWERFUL TOOL—USE IT

"Every brain is a broadcasting and receiving station for the vibrations of thought."
~ **Napoleon Hill**

Our brains are incredibly complex organs—far more powerful than even the most advanced computers. The thoughts we think have tremendous potential: They can set goals, pursue them, and achieve them. Whether climbing mountains, founding a business, or solving complicated mathematical proofs, our brains and thoughts are propelling us there.

In fact, *every single decision* we make throughout our day is guided by our brains: From the smallest, like taking a single breath, to the largest, like whether or not to close a major deal.

Put Your Brain to Work

The brain has immense potential, but that doesn't guarantee that we're always tapping into it. Indeed, we often squander our mind's potential. So, what can we do to prevent this?

One technique to practice is brainstorming. This is a surefire way to hone your thinking. It requires deep concentration, a sense of purpose, and engaging with other people—and minds—around you. It keeps you active, sharp, and alert.

This last part—engaging with other people—is essential. Brains are often likened to computers, but they can also be compared to radios: "They are broadcasting and receiving stations for the vibration of thought," Napoleon Hill wrote.

Hill believed that others could pick up the vibrations our brains put out into the world. He also believed that "what you attract is a result of what you vibrate." If your brain vibrates positive thoughts and desires, you'll bring good people and things into your orbit.

I have an anecdote that exemplifies the benefits of brainstorming and positive vibrations. It's the story of a client, a novel idea, a senior care facility, and a big marketing success.

In my business, creativity is key. Our role as marketing and PR professionals is to help our clients stand out amid the clutter and the noise. When tasked with a project, we are not simply a set of hands; we need to dial up our brain power and creativity. So, when a client of mine —the CEO of a sizable senior-living campus—came to me wanting to make a splash, I knew I had to get creative.

The client approached me to write a news release announcing an online program for seniors in partnership with a local university. Essentially, college students were coming to the facility to help seniors seventy and above navigate the internet, connect with their grandchildren, use email, and more. In my mind, I knew that if we sent out this announcement as-is, it would get very little play in the media. After all, many similar programs were being offered to seniors around the region.

I told the client to give me a day or two, and I'd get back to her with some recommendations. And after brainstorming, I landed on the breakthrough idea: Create a graduation ceremony following the 13-week program. Seniors would traverse the stage—by walker, wheelchair, or their own sturdy legs—to receive course completion certificates from the college students. The cost? A sheet cake and some fruit punch.

The CEO instantly loved it—especially the affordability angle since the organization was a non-profit. She also agreed to the suggestion of inviting the seniors' family and staff. Ultimately, we received broadcast and front-page coverage—a big success. But it went much deeper, too, touching staff, seniors, families, college students, and college faculty. Making this idea come to life was one of the most joyous moments in my career. To see the proud smiles on the seniors' faces as they accepted the certificates will forever be ingrained in my mind and heart.

And take note: *All* of this—the marketing success, the beautiful memories—started with a brainstorm.

Take Care of Your Brain

It's crystal clear how integral and how indispensable the brain is. So, how can you ensure you're taking good care of it?

To start, don't take it for granted. Like any other part of your body, it requires the right kind of care and stimulation if you expect it to be creative, productive, and perform at its peak. Here are eight ways to do just that:

Get a Good Night's Sleep

This is essential. Countless studies—and plenty of anecdotal evidence—show that sleep is critical for brain health. It allows your brain to rest and repair itself. Consistently aim for seven to eight hours of sleep per night. And make sure it's quality sleep, too: no interruptions. Close the shades, turn off the lights, and put the phone on silent.

Eat a Healthy Diet

Like the rest of your body, your brain needs the right nutrients to function properly. Eating a healthy diet with plenty of fruits, vegetables, and whole grains will help keep your brain healthy. Have you ever skipped the healthy stuff and found your mind feeling foggy? That's all the proof you need that your brain deserves a balanced diet.

Exercise Regularly

Exercise has numerous benefits for brain health. It improves blood flow, reduces inflammation, lowers stress, and releases powerful, positive chemicals like endorphins. Aim for a minimum of thirty minutes of moderate exercise most days of the week. Jogging, swimming, and weightlifting are all great habits to get into.

Challenge Your Mind

To keep our lungs and legs healthy, we run. To keep our arms healthy, we curl weights. What about our brains? Mental exercises are just as important as physical ones. Make time every day for activities like crossword puzzles and memory games. Complicated card games are excellent, too, like bridge. Learning a new skill can also keep your brain sharp, especially as you age—so maybe it's time to take up Sudoku.

Experience New Things

When you get out of your comfort zone and embark on a new adventure, you're also pushing your brain in a new direction. New opportunities provide new perspectives and supple ground for ideation and creativity. So, plan a trip to a new country. Take a performing arts, writing, or painting class. And teach yourself how to do your own taxes.

Become a Lifelong Learner

You may have finished your formal education in high school or college, but that's no excuse to stop learning. Successful people are obsessed with learning. Train yourself to always be curious. And always ask questions: *Why? Where? How? What? Who?* If there are things or events that you need help understanding, try to expand your knowledge and skills with books, podcasts, YouTube, online courses, and more.

Inject Play into Your Life

I have a confession. I love Legos. Any chance I get, I will buy them as a gift for friends or family with kids—and then politely remove myself from the "adult" room to play with them for a bit. There's a playful "builder" in me and always has been: I fondly recall my love growing up for Mr. Potato head and swapping different body parts to make new creations. These days, I still play games. My favorite? Scrabble. The point here is to embrace imaginative play as an escape. It requires you to see things differently, which is the essence of igniting your brain power.

Connect with Others

Last, but not least, is social interaction. Relationships are imperative for brain health, as it helps to keep your mind active and engaged. Make an effort to connect with family and friends regularly, even if it's just a phone call while walking the dog.

As you pursue your dreams and goals, make sure you're both leveraging and taking good care of your most important asset: your brain. Everything starts with the mind—so keep your thoughts trained on positivity and prosperity.

STACEY ROSS COHEN

About Stacey Ross Cohen: In the world of branding, few experts possess the savvy and instinct of Stacey. An award-winning brand professional who earned her stripes on Madison Avenue and major television networks before launching her own agency, Stacey specializes in cultivating and amplifying brands.

Stacey is CEO of Co-Communications, a marketing agency headquartered in New York. She coaches businesses and individuals across a range of industries — from real estate to healthcare and education—and expertly positions their narratives in fiercely competitive markets.

A TEDx speaker, Stacey is a sought-after keynote at industry conferences and author in the realm of branding, PR, and marketing. She is a contributor at Huffington Post and Thrive Global and has been featured in *Forbes, Entrepreneur, Crain's* and a suite of other media outlets. She holds a B.S. from Syracuse University, MBA from Fordham University and a certificate in Media, Technology and Entertainment from NYU Stern School of Business.

Author's Website: *www.StaceyRossCohen.com*

Book Series Website: *www.The13StepsToRiches.com*

Teresa Cundiff

THE MYSTERIOUS BRAIN

Brain freeze, scatter-brained, pick your brain, brainwashed, wrap your brain around it, brain like a sieve, wrack your brain, brainwave, brain is fried, brain dead, brain dump, brain fart, brain trust, no-brainer, brain food, tax your brain, hair-brained, all brawn and no brain, bird-brain, beat your brains out/in, brain cramp, brain drain, brainstorm, brains versus brawn, brain-teaser, lamebrain, mommy brain, two brains are better than one, the brains behind something, and the classic shit for brains!

Who knew that we use the word brain so much? And that is not even an exhaustive list! In a survey from 2013, 65% of Americans believed that we only use 10% of our brains! This has been debunked, however, as discussed in an interview with Dr. Barry Gordon in Scientific America! We use most of our brain most of the time even when performing a very simple action! Given that the brain only weighs about three pounds, it's incredible that it contains 100 billion neurons. All this information came from Medical News Today, February 27, 2018.

I, for one, am pleased to know that I use most of my brain! Being blonde, I get all the blonde jokes, so it was comforting to learn that maybe there was more brain capacity for us blondes, but alas, the facts speak for themselves!

The brain is very mysterious as it does so many things automatically that we take for granted. The story of my brain came to the fore around Christmas 2017. My older son, John, wanted a hammock for Christmas to add to his camping gear. I was like, "I need to get John's hammock

254

ordered," and sat down at the computer and ordered it. Then the next day I was like, "I need to get John's hammock ordered," and sat down at the computer and ordered it! Yep! That's right! I ordered two hammocks just one day apart because I didn't remember ordering it just one day before!

The next rather serious brain mishap also involved money! I paid off a credit card because I was going to put a vehicle repair on it. So, my car goes in the shop, I pay for it with the aforementioned credit card and go on about my day. Some time goes by, and I get a bill from the credit card company. I am indignant that they are sending me a bill because I paid that card off!

Yep, you guessed it! I didn't remember paying for the car repair with the card! I'm talking the whole transaction of putting my car in and getting it out of the shop! Clearly, this whole situation was getting serious since now I am spending money and not recalling making the purchases. This drove me immediately to the doctor. Time to figure out what was going on in my brain.

My doctor is awesome and told me I should see a neurologist. So, I make that appointment which leads to an EEG (electro encephalogram) to check the electrical stuff going on. Normal. I also take a bunch of cognitive tests in the office to which I scored the highest of everyone in my age category! Awesome right? Except we are still searching for what is going on with my memory! Then comes the MRI!

It's the first brain MRI I have ever had. In case you've never seen an MRI machine in person or on TV, it's like a giant white donut and you are the donut hole! The room temperature is freezing to accommodate the machine. Who cares about the people? It's all about the machine not overheating.

The technicians where I go for imaging are super! They place a triangular wedge under my knees to take the pressure off my lower back when I lie down. They give me earplugs because, oh my goodness, is that thing loud! Next, my head gets put in a harness of sorts to keep it perfectly still while the machine pounds me with magnetic stuff and a cage is placed over my face. Lastly, they cover me up with lots of blankets because it takes a while to map the brain. When the imaging is over, the report gets sent to the doctor. And finally, I have my diagnosis.

I don't know if it has a fancy doctor name or not. I can't remember, LOL! But the long and short of it was that blood wasn't flowing to the very end of the little capillaries in my brain. They were stuck and not pulsating with my heartbeat! Amazing! So, with that information, the doctor put me on a drug that's used for migraines at the highest dose allowed! He said that the drug only worked for 20% of the people that he prescribed it to for memory loss. And let me tell you, that drug changed my life!

As the dosage was building up in my system, I could feel things landing in my brain like a card dropping into a slot. It was incredible to be able to recall things again instead of always having to say, "I don't remember." So, fast forward to now, and my current neurologist is concerned about the high dosage of the medication and has had me ween off it.

I will confess that I'm not excited about this, but he tells me that high doses of the drug can cause cognitive failure. So, I am left in a catch-22…continue taking the drug to have a memory now or stop taking the drug to avoid future cognitive failure! It's a dilemma.

So, why have I told you this very personal story? Because for all that modern medicine knows about the brain, there is still more for them to learn. My case is just one and the right course of action is unsure due to the fact that my neurologist can't predict the future. My brain will do what it will do, as will yours.

In reading Napoleon Hill's chapter on the brain in *Think and Grow Rich*, I am constantly fascinated by the discipline he exercises over his brain! He had imaginary council meetings with the likes of Lincoln and Edison! He once had a tooth extracted without anesthesia and avoided processing the pain by just thinking that he was in a hall giving a lecture!

He mastered his brain like no other! Hill states that, "Every human brain is capable of picking up vibrations of thought which are being released by other brains." He goes on to explain that those vibrations must be attached to an emotion so that the vibrations are occurring at a very high level. He likens it to a mental broadcasting system. And, again as a blonde, it's great to learn that my brain can pick stuff up from other people's brains! Ba-dump-bump!

I know that when my own brain is struggling to remember, I wish that there was someone around to help me by giving off vibrations from their brain! But I don't dwell on the fact that I'm currently suffering from memory loss. It has been definitively stated that I do not have Alzheimer's which is a blessing. I have been through another battery of tests with the neuropsychologist to get my baseline brain function with a new EEG as well. I don't know if a new MRI will be ordered.

I am thankful for Hill's book where he offers so much practical information through his thirteen principles. Because of him, we can study *Think and Grow Rich* and apply his thoughts to our own. He brings fresh insight and understanding to the subconscious mind and the Master Mind that all of this stimulates my mind. Never underestimate the power of reading and studying literature that will allow you to grow and develop.

As I interview authors on my TV show Teresa Talks, I read each book from cover to cover. It has forced me to read books I might not otherwise have picked up, and I'm all the better for it! My brain is better for it! Books are powerful things because they contain the thoughts of the author on a subject! Or the book can be a collaboration like this one where 33 different people get to tell you what they think about the brain! This is all for your consideration, dear reader, to use and apply as you see fit. Always be reading something at any given time! Do whatever you can to keep your brain fit and healthy!

More mysteries are being unlocked about the brain and all it can do! All well and good but use the one you have to make good decisions and seek your Mastermind group when you need counsel. Two heads are better than one can be restated as two brains are better than one!

TERESA CUNDIFF

About Teresa Cundiff: Teresa hosts an interview digital TV show called Teresa Talks on Legrity TV. On the show, she interviews authors who are published and unpublished—and that just means those authors haven't put their books on paper yet. The show provides a platform for authors to have a global reach with their message. Teresa Talks is produced by Wordy Nerds Media Inc., of which Cundiff is the CEO.

Cundiff is also a freelance proofreader with the tagline, "I know where the commas go!" Teresa makes her clients work shine with her knowledge of grammar, punctuation, and sentence structure.

Teresa is a four-time international bestselling contributing author of 1 Habit for Entrepreneurial Success, 1 Habit to Thrive in a Post-COVID World, The Art of Connection: 365 Days of Networking Quotes and The Art of Connection: 365 Days of Inspirational Quotes. The latter two are both placed in the Library of Congress. She is a ten-time bestselling contributing author to *The 13 Steps to Riches* Series.

Author's Website: *www.TeresaTalksTv.com*

Book Series Website: *www.The13StepsToRiches.com*

Vera Thomas

BRAIN HEALTH—BRAIN WEALTH

The mind and the brain are not the same.
There is no mind without a brain.
There is no brain ability without the function of the mind.
A proven fact by studies time after time
Unconscious or conscious the mind has a say.
The brain controls the functions we display.
Every nerve, cell, tissue, vein, organ,
and emotion is controlled by the brain.
Our mind determines what we claim.
Our children reflect the same.

Napoleon Hill titles the brain chapter as, "*The Brain: A Broadcasting and Receiving Station for Thought.*" Since the writing of *Think and Grow Rich*, there have been extensive studies of the brain and the power of the mind and the correlation between the two.

In addition to the natural condition of both the brain and the mind, we now have AI to contend with and consider as a component to imitate, enhance, and possibly control how our mind and brain function. While AI is not my topic for discussion, I thought I would mention it as something to be considered as to how it will impact our brains and our society now and in the near future.

We know that the brain controls every aspect of our physical being; our minds can determine how well our brain serve us. "Healthy mind connotes a healthy brain." Our health can determine both our minds and our brains.

According to Harvard Health Publishing, Harvard Medical School (May 13, 2022). there are 12 ways to keep your brain young. Given my age, I find this article of importance and worth expounding upon in this chapter.

Get Mental Stimulation

As I have said in the past, "We are either green and growing or ripe and rotten." We cannot expect our brains to remain healthy if we are not willing to feed it mentally through a variety of stimuli. In fact, according to the article, research with mice and humans indicate mental stimuli may "increase new connections between nerve cells and may even help the brain generate new cells, developing neurological "plasticity" and building up a functional reserve that provides a hedge against future cell loss." Puzzles, reading, taking classes, using your creativity like drawing, writing, painting can all contribute to mental stimulation.

For me, being a poet and committing poetry to memory is one of the methods I use. I love, value, and appreciate all aspects of the arts and wish I could paint, but given that I cannot draw straight lines, appreciating the works of others is as far as that kind of creativity goes for me. Discover your creativity, revisit the chapter on Creativity; better yet, get the *13 Steps to Riches* series and revisit the book on creativity as a resource for further developing your creativity to stimulate your brain.

Get Physical Exercise

I must admit, this has not been an area of strength for me. Growing up, I was the child others would say, "Do we have to have her on our team?" Even as an adult, wanting to participate in baseball, volleyball, or anything to do with a ball, for instance, our church outings, after volunteering to be on a team, I would politely be told, "Vera, it is all right; you do not have to play! See where else you might be useful!"

I have had several accidents over the years that caused arthritis in both my knees. It was not until just recently when arthritis in both my knees had gotten so bad, I was hardly able to walk, and I realized the importance of exercise! After X-rays of both my knees, the orthopedic doctor said to me, "It is amazing you have been able to walk at all!" Clearly, we lose what we do not use!

After cortisone shots in both my knees, I walk! The effects of the shots will last for the next three months. I will eventually need knee surgery. In the meantime, I walk! Physical exercise is absolutely necessary, not only for our bodies but for our brains as well. In fact, exercise can help with other conditions on this list.

Improve Your Diet

This is an area I am very intentional about. I believe what I have heard, "We are what we eat!" Our diet can not only enhance our brain; it can improve other things that are on this list. I do not believe in taking medications. Even with the excruciating pain from arthritis in my knees, I avoided taking medication on a regular basis because of the side effects. We take medication for one condition and in most cases, it impacts on other areas of our health. I believe our diets can help most reasons for medication and possibly eliminate medications altogether.

The article suggests that a Mediterranean diet provides food for the brain. Nuts, fruit, vegetables, olive oil, fish, and plant-based proteins stimulate the brain. My diet primarily consists of these things. I love salmon and could possibly eat it every day cooked in a variety of ways. I love beans. I found a recipe for black beans that included sweet potatoes; I added chicken and let me tell you, it was delicious! I avoid fried foods as much as possible. Chicken, fish, and turkey are my mainstays.

I believe my diet is one of my saving graces. I will be 70 this year and not on any medications. I do contribute much of that to my diet.

Improve Your Blood Pressure

Our diets and exercise, or lack thereof, have much to do with our blood pressure. According to the article, high blood pressure affects our cognitive ability. A couple of years ago, my doctor suggested that I may need to start taking blood pressure medication because my blood pressure was borderline high. My first question to her was, "What can I do naturally to avoid medication?"

My doctor is from India, and one of the things she indicated is that turmeric is a staple in her culture and high blood pressure is not the norm. I started taking turmeric daily, either by putting it in my food, taking what is called turmeric shots (a small bottle that can be found at any health food store) and I did get the capsules. My blood pressure is now normal and high blood pressure medication is no longer an option!

How we handle stress can also impact on our blood pressure. Remember, there is good stress and bad stress—how we react, relate, and respond to stressors can impact on our cognitive function. Learning to change things we can, accept things we cannot change and knowing the difference can help when dealing with stress.

Improve Your Blood Sugar

Diabetes is running rampant in our country and at early ages. According to the Center for Disease Control, "Diagnosed cases of type 1 and type 2 diabetes are surging among youth in the United States. From 2001 to 2017, the number of people under age 20 living with type 1 diabetes increased by 45%, and the number living with type 2 diabetes grew by 95%."

The estimated number of youths aged 0-19 years with type 1 diabetes increased from 148 per 100,000 in 2001 to 215 per 100,000 in 2017. These statistics are dated, yet there is no reason to assume they have decreased. It is particularly of great concern among African Americans and Hispanics.

Diabetes is a contributing factor for dementia. Again, our diets, exercise and weight control have much to do with our blood sugar level. White sugar is poison to our brain and body in general. We cannot help but have it as it is in almost everything, particularly processed foods. Other causes include obesity and lack of physical activity, insulin resistance, genetics, family history of diabetes and ethnicity.

Given my platform is dealing with children and their parents, I want to include signs parents can be aware of that your child may be at risk.

- Low Temperature
- Loss of Balance
- Slow Reflexes
- Tiredness
- Nausea and Vomiting
- Irritability (that is out of the norm due to other symptoms) in teens
- Blurry Vision
- Increased Thirst
- Increased Urination

Improve your cholesterol. Bad cholesterol level can increase dementia. A couple of years ago, this too was an issue that was of concern to my doctor. My bad cholesterol levels needed to improve. Again, my question, "What can I do naturally?" She suggested eliminating some things from my diet and losing a few pounds could help. I took heed and started eating Cheerios on a regular basis. I am not on medication for this.

Time does not permit me to expound on the other things to consider for brain health. I have included them for your consideration:

- **Consider Low-Dose Aspirin**
- **Avoid Tobacco**
- **Do Not Abuse Alcohol**
- **Care for Your Emotions**

- **Protect Your Head**
- **Build Social Networks**

Remember, things we can do to sustain a healthy brain and mind. We have more control than we often want to admit.

References

Harvard Health Publishing, Harvard Medical School (May 13, 2022) *https://www.health.harvard.edu/mind-and-mood/12-ways-to-keep-your-brain-young*

Center for Disease Control, www.cdc.gov

Diabetic News, https://diabetic.news/9-signs-symptoms-diabetes-children/

VERA THOMAS

About Vera Thomas: Vera Thomas lives in the state of Georgia. She is, to date, a four-time Bestselling Author, podcast host, certified transformation coach, family mediator, and a Classroom Management Advocate, Trainer, Speaker, and Poet. She works with parents, children, schools, organizations and churches.

Vera's life story directed her towards work with organizations that provided hope and empowerment to people like her to better themselves. It is her goal to help others overcome a circumstance that diminishes and help them to surge ahead with their dreams. Vera graduated "Cum Laude" with a Bachelor's in psychology from Walsh University in Canton, OH.

Vera's work as a facilitator for more than three decades and includes developing training programs for youth and adults. Hear her story and think about your own. Vera is available for companies who want to transform their teams or individuals who want to transform their lives.

Author's Website: *www.linktr.ee/VeraThomasInstillingGreatness*

Book Series Website: *www.The13StepsToRiches.com*

Yuri Choi

THE BRAIN ATTRACTS

Recently, I was listening to an old *School of Greatness* podcast episode where Lewis Howes was interviewing the late legend, Bob Proctor. I am sure you know Bob Proctor as he was when he had already become well-known and the great teacher that he was, but did you know that he used to be broke, unhealthy, and felt very lost during his younger years for a long time? It wasn't until he found a mentor who helped him with changing his mindset and his perception about what's possible that he started to become successful. (And, in fact, the book that he was told to read at the time by his mentor was *Think and Grow Rich,* and Bob credits this book as a crucial ingredient for his success.)

In this interview, Bob talked about something very specific that he did that changed his life. He mentioned that, upon the recommendation of his mentor, he started to carry a golden notecard with his financial goals handwritten on it. Bob explained that this simple act of writing down his goal and carrying it everywhere with him helped him intentionally focus on and give energy to his goal every day.

By having this on his mind and also having the physical reminder of it at all times, he started to attract more opportunities that would help him get to his goals in a miraculously short amount of time. The reason, he explained, was because by thinking about this burning desire he had of his financial goal every day, he was actually starting to *notice, pay attention to,* or *hear* opportunities, connections, or resources that would help him get to his financial goals faster. And Bob explained that this was really the starting point of when he started to understand how laws of attraction was working for him.

And, by the way, we have all experienced this in the past whether you are actively aware of this or not at this moment as you read this story about Bob, and whether you subscribe to the idea of laws of attraction or not. Do you remember that one time you were trying to buy a specific car, you all of the sudden started to notice that car everywhere you go? For example, imagine that you had wanted to buy a red convertible, you might start to notice more red convertibles more than ever, people who own them, or people who also want them. Or what about that one time you wanted to buy a specific brand bag or shoes, and all of the sudden, you start to notice them everywhere.

While the concept of *laws of attraction* seems very "out there" and "woo-woo" for some, this mechanism that highlights our ability to scan our environment for what we are focusing on so we can find what we want easier, while filtering out the irrelevant information, is actually a very much grounded neuroscientific system that is built in all of us. This system is called *reticular activating system* (RAS). This could potentially be considered a survival mechanism of the brain that allows us to look for the food that we need, look for danger we can run away from and protect our children from, and so on.

For instance, there was a study done where they had moms and their babies in another section of a very loud plane. They found that when babies in the next room started crying, moms picked up the sound, even in their sleep! As you can see, this makes sense because to a mom of a newborn, the thought of their babies' safety and well-being is at the top of their mind.

And while everyone, including newborns' moms, have over 60 to 80,000 thoughts a day automatically without trying, and we are all constantly bombarded by different sensory input from our environments, it is through our *RAS* hard at work, that allows humans to be extra selective about what actually gets our attention to take action. *RAS* essentially filters out less prioritized thoughts, so we can pay attention to the ones that matter.

As a performance coach for high achievers and entrepreneurs, this is a brain mechanism I often explain to my clients, and it helps them greatly.

This is because when the logical mind can understand the function behind our *RAS* is mixed with practicing an intentional abundant mindset, where my clients are actually designing what they *want,* rather than what they *need* to merely survive, it helps them understand why keeping our visualizations, affirmations, and our burning desires at the top of our minds, can be extremely powerful. This helps us get more of what we want, and it allows the Universe to work for us, easier.

This seems rather obvious at a glance, right? "Think about what you want." How hard could that possibly be?

You'd be surprised how often people *think* they are thinking about what they want, but, in reality, they are actually thinking about what they don't want. For instance, one of my clients once said she wanted to eliminate her debt. When I asked her to create a customized affirmation around this, she wrote down, "I will eliminate my debt by the end of my 3 months coaching program working with Yuri."

While I was happy that she was very specific and clear about her goals, there was one problem based on what we now know regarding the *reticular activating system.* She was focusing on the word "debt," which was actually something she wanted to *eliminate,* not attract. I challenged her with this question, "Can you re-write this goal in a way that you aren't using the word related to what you don't want?" And at first, my client was confused. "But that *is* what I want!" And I told her, "Yes it is, in a way, but what gets to happen so that you can truly eliminate your debt?"

She thought for a moment, and we went back and forth for a few moments. Finally, she got it! She exclaimed, "I guess I would want to attract $20,000 into my bank account!" Yes! Although the technical "outcome" of this goal might seem very similar on the surface, it completely changed what her brain would be scanning her environment for. She was now set to either consciously or subconsciously look for opportunities that would invite more money into her account, rather than keep attracting the energy of *debt.*

I've learned to leverage what I know about the reticular activating system as well. For instance, I get very clear about who I want to attract into my life as clients. Instead of focusing on what I don't want, I focus on what I want in my soul-level clients.

An example of writing down what I don't want would sound something like, "I don't want clients who are lazy, pessimistic about the process, and those who are rude." And if I were to affirm this, I would be attracting exactly what I don't want because of the language I am using. It would allow my brain to scan for those who are lazy, pessimistic, and rude, even if I said *"not those."* The brain doesn't know the difference.

And so instead, I would affirm something like this, "I am excited and grateful to attract dedicated, optimistic, and those who are in integrity as my clients." Now, my brain would be automatically focusing on the frequency around these words that I just said out loud.

While many initially might think that spirituality and neuroscience are separate, the more and more we find out about our brains' mechanisms and how it works, we are finding more and more that they are intertwined than not. And even if you are a spiritual entrepreneur as I am, you might benefit (and your logical side) from understanding the scientific mechanism of why holding a burning desire, being selective and intentional about what thoughts we give energy to, and how we attract these things we want into our lives can amplify the effects of what is already at work.

While these laws of the Universe are working with or without your knowledge of them (such as how gravity is working whether we know how it works or not), it absolutely offers a foundation for our left brain to get grounded in these facts for our heart and our creative side of our brains to digest better.

Knowing more about your brain now, you powerful being, what will you start to give energy to so you can attract, create and manifest more into your life and business? What visions and goals get to be at the forefront of your mind? What burning desires will you nurture and give energy to by focusing on them?

Journaling Questions:

1. When was a time in your own life or in business where you noticed that the *reticular activating system* of your brain was working for you?

2. Can you think of a time that you had very vivid visions or burning desires around what you truly wanted to attract into your life, and it happened? What happened?

3. What are your current burning desires that you can give energy to every day for the next 7 days?

YURI CHOI

About Yuri Choi: Yuri is Founder of Yuri Choi Coaching. Choi is a performance coach for entrepreneurs and high achievers. She helps them create and stay in a powerful, abundant, unstoppable mindset to achieve their goals by helping them gain clarity and understanding, leverage their emotional states, and create empowering habits and language patterns.

She is a speaker, writer, creator, connector, YouTuber, and the author of Creating Your Own Happiness. Choi is passionate about spreading the messages about meditation, power of intention, and creating a powerful mindset to live a fulfilling life. She is also a Habitude Warrior Conference Speaker and emcee, and she is also a designated guest coach for Psych2Go, the largest online mental health magazine and YouTube Channel.

Her mission in the world is to inspire people to live leading with L.O.V.E. (which stands for: laughter, oneness, vulnerability, and ease) and to ignite people's souls to live in a world of infinite creative possibilities and abundance.

Author's Website: www.YuriChoiCoaching.com

Book Series Website: *www.The13StepsToRiches.com*

GRAB YOUR COPY OF AN OFFICIAL PUBLICATION
WITH THE ORIGINAL UNEDITED TEXT FROM 1937
BY THE NAPOLEON HILL FOUNDATION!

THE NAPOLEON HILL FOUNDATION
WWW.NAPHILL.ORG

HABITUDE WARRIOR & INTEGRITY PUBLISHING EDITORIAL TEAM

Habitude Warrior International and Integrity Publishing take great pride in our editorial team who put their sweat, tears, and heart into each and every project and national bestseller! Thank you team!

JON KOVACH JR.
Team Manager

Jon Kovach Jr. strives to assist every author and every team member in the process of self-development for ultimate success.

PAT MINTON
VP of Operations

Pat Minton has been with the Habitude Warrior International team for over 20 years getting her start with Brian Tracy & Erik Swanson.

JILLIAN KOVACH
Editorial Manager

Jillian is a vital team member of Habitude Warrior & Integrity Publishing bringing her expertise managing our Editorial Department.

FATIMA HURD
Editorial Team & Photographer

Fatima is our Professional Photographer for Habitude Warrior as well as one of our members on the Proofing Department team.

LAUREN COBB
Editorial Team Member

Lauren Cobb is part of our Proofing Department for Habitude Warrior & Integrity Publishing as well as one of our authors.

To inquire about joining our team please send us an email to Team@HabitudeWarrior.com

www.ingramcontent.com/pod-product-compliance
Lightning Source LLC
Chambersburg PA
CBHW051300120626
46547CB00015B/2025